Relationship Restored

"Whether you agree or disagree with Smartt's conclusions, his book will surely challenge and inspire you—challenge your assumptions about the divisions of church polity and inspire you toward greater unity in Christ. Smartt pursues a form of ecclesiastical ecumenism without squishy platitudes and avoiding real doctrinal clarity. His work is rooted in clear biblical exegesis and historical wisdom for practical answers in church life today."

—**Robbie Crouse**, Professor of Systematic Theology, Knox Theological Seminary

"Nick Smartt's *Relationship Restored* is a thoughtful and hopeful call for unity grounded in God's covenantal grace rather than human effort. He reminds us that faith is God's gift, not our achievement, and that the church's oneness flows from Christ's promises fulfilled in word and sacrament. While readers may differ on particulars, Smartt's irenic spirit and deep love for Christ's church invite all who grieve its divisions to see again the beauty of belonging to one body under one Lord."

—**Orrey McFarland**, Pastor, Peace Lutheran Church, Edmond, Oklahoma

"Nick Smartt addresses one of the critical issues in the church today, namely, how to find unity in the midst of the diversity of denominations and theological emphases in Christianity. Highlighting this major challenge is cause enough for engaging with this book. While Smartt focuses on unity among evangelicals within the reformed tradition, many of the insights are sure to spark conversations that are relevant to the larger Christian family as well."

—**Bill Warren**, Director, Center for New Testament Textual Studies, New Orleans Baptist Theological Seminary

"In an age when we see so much division, the church needs unity like that for which Nick Smartt calls. May this book prompt many much-needed discussions in that direction."

—**Elijah Hixson**, Postdoctoral Research Fellow, New Orleans Baptist Theological Seminary

"In this intriguing work, Nick Smartt provides a way to move towards evangelical reunion. As Christians living in the modern West, we face many enemies. . . . If our divisions continue, we will fall, but united in the core truths of the gospel we can stand firm. *Relationship Restored* is a timely and important call to unite around core doctrines, make room for reasonable diversity in disputed secondary practices, and regain the church's power as a cultural force for good."

—**Rich Lusk**, Pastor, Trinity Presbyterian Church, Birmingham, Alabama

Relationship Restored

A Plea for Reconciliation Among Conservative Evangelical Churches

Nick S. Smartt

WIPF & STOCK · Eugene, Oregon

Wipf & Stock
An Imprint of Wipf and Stock Publishers
199 W. 8th Ave., Suite 3
Eugene, OR 97401

www.wipfandstock.com

PAPERBACK ISBN: 979-8-3852-6372-1
HARDCOVER ISBN: 979-8-3852-6373-8
EBOOK ISBN: 979-8-3852-6374-5

VERSION NUMBER 12/02/25

To my bride Heather

You look for redemption in every area of life and offer a helping hand at all times in order to be a part of that redemptive process. Without you life would be colorless, but with you it is vibrant.

I do not ask for these only, but also for those who will believe in me through their word, that they may all be one, just as you, Father, are in me, and I in you, that they also may be in us, so that the world may believe that you have sent me.

—Jesus in John 17:20–21

Contents

Preface

THIS BOOK IS THE product of personal experiences mixed with course work during the completion of my master of divinity degree at Knox Theological Seminary. Over the span of three years I had the privilege to study under Dr. Robbie Crouse, who allowed me to craft coursework toward my own church situation. Due to his oversight and direction, this work was a combination of various course studies culminating in my graduate thesis. Therefore, this book will float somewhere between popular and academic writing. Though terms are meant to be understood by most pastors and laypeople, some may come across as overly academic. Nonetheless the intention has always been for this book to find its way into the practical outworkings of the church.

First and foremost, this book is indicative of my personal experience with the church. If I were cornered and commanded to give my denominational guild then I would identify myself as exegetically Reformed, sacramentally Lutheran, ecclesiastically Episcopalian, and missionally Baptist. There you have it. I am a Reformed Luthbaptalian. Thus you can understand my desire to unite various sects of conservative evangelicalism. Too many experiences of mine have formed my mindset that there is more in common between us than there is different. Along with that, I have seen opportunities vanquished because of doctrinal squabbles that amount to a hill of beans. The reader should not be led to believe that I am apathetic toward doctrine or the weighty matters of debate. I would consider my continual pursuit of studies as evidence to the contrary. However, I do believe that such doctrinal hostilities are given too much spotlight in consideration of the far greater matters with which all these parties agree. And it is because of this that the present work is submitted to the reader.

Finally, it would only be fitting to affirm what I wish to have acknowledged many years ago. In the pursuit of further study and understanding of God's word, very few doctrines are set in stone as "untouchable." As Irenaeus of Lyons alluded to in his writing, the core doctrines of orthodoxy should be very small because the truth of the Bible is inexhaustible and its enemies innumerable. Therefore I end this preface with an ear open to critique and a mind open to change, so long as that change stems from a valid reading of God's inspired word.

Introduction

THERE ARE TWO THREADS that I hope to weave together within this book. The first thread has a vertical disposition that will convey how God restores relationship with his people throughout redemptive history by the means of covenant. The second thread has a horizontal disposition that hopes to restore the relationship between two competing sects within the conservative evangelical tradition—namely, that of the credo and paedo factions.[1] Whether it is a credobaptist versus a paedobaptist or a credocommunist versus a paedocommunist, the practices of the two holy ordinances of the church have driven a wedge between otherwise like-minded brothers and sisters.[2]

This regrettable infighting within the church is personal to me, as I have been on the front lines of such a division, not just within my church, but within my own marriage. After being a member at a Presbyterian church I met my Baptist wife with

1. Please note that this does not intend to address the same ecumenical desire proposed by theological liberals such as those noted in the National Council of Churches, World Council of Churches, Consultation on Church Union, etc. This is an argument for ecumenical unity between evangelical churches—namely, those who believe that God's inspired word ought to rule every aspect of their lives.

2. Paedo=child; credo=creed. Thus a paedocommunist is someone who promotes giving the ordinance of the Lord's Supper (communion) to young children despite them not having a "reputable" creed. Admittedly, paedocommunion is a rare opinion, but I hope to show its validity throughout the rest of the book.

whom I fell deeply in love. After our wedding day we committed to finding a church that loved the Lord, and to submitting to its authority on all things, including its practice of baptism. Due to the obvious expression of Christian love within its doors, we settled on the church just down the street in which she was already a member. My wife testified to her increasing maturity in the faith as a result of this church's ministry. So I made the difficult decision to remove myself from membership within my Presbyterian church in order to commit to serving and loving this Baptist church. Regrettably, because of different perspectives on baptism I was an orphan sheep of Christ's flock, being denied membership to this church for seven and a half years. After one conversation with my wife about this topic of baptism and the denial of my church membership she lamented, "I just feel alone." In no small manner, this restriction became a threat to the unity of my marriage. How many other Christians "just feel alone" when experiencing disunity with other brothers and sisters in Christ over this topic? For my marriage and for many brothers and sisters across denominational lines, the differences on how to handle the ordinances of the church have produced many tears and sleepless nights, and it has extinguished opportunities for love. I denounce this disunity with the likes of Francis Turretin who remarked, "We cannot behold without grief that those things which were instituted by God to be bonds and symbols of union and concord among Christians, have been made the seed plot of contentions and the apple of discord."[3] More recently, Murray echoed a similar refrain:

> It is to be admitted that the fragmentation and lack of coordination and solidarity which we find within strictly evangelical and Reformed Churches creates a difficult situation, and how this disunity is to be remedied is a task not easily accomplished. But what needs to be indicted, and indicted with vehemence, is the complacency so widespread, and the failure to be aware that this is an evil, dishonoring to Christ, destructive of the edification

---

3. Turretin, *Institutes*, 3:337.

defined by the apostles, and prejudicial to the evangelistic outreach to the world.[4]

The ecumenical scholar John Frame succinctly concludes that "the
birth of a denomination is always attended by sin."[5]

Some may think that these denominational divisions on
non-fundamental issues are necessary and helpful for unity and
peace within the church, but I am not one of them. Certainly
denominations allow "for amicable, civilized divorces among
believers."[6] But this "divorce" is something the church should not
advocate nor desire because God did not intend for schisms in
his bride. Anyone from a divorced family like myself can attest
that divorce is painful and not the original intention of God. I
have benefited much from the love of my Baptist brethren who
take the gospel seriously and "walk the walk" of the Christian life.
My Baptist brothers and sisters are incredibly pious and zealously
evangelical. Thus, I want more Christians to be challenged and
benefited through this type of cross-pollination that rarely exists in this denominationally crazed evangelical world. The words
"Let your kingdom come on earth as it is in heaven" (see Matt
6:9–15) are not hollow for me, but a real expression of my desire
to see unity within the church on earth in order that it might
reflect the perfect unity of our heavenly congregation.

While I am not naive to think that my writing will be enough
to change the tide of disunity within the church, perhaps it may
change the minds of a few saints. Perhaps there will be more understanding between those of differing opinions. Perhaps some
within one faction will start to see those "on the other side" not
as enemies but as brothers and sisters with whom they can commune in the same church family. In short, perhaps this assessment may be helpful to a few. And it is those few, grieving with
me about this disunity and earnestly desiring a unifying path
forward, to whom I write.

4. Murray, *Select Lectures*, 335.
5. Frame, *Evangelical Reunion*, 23.
6. Frame, *Evangelical Reunion*, 40.

Therefore, as a possible mediating ethic by which conservative evangelical Christians from different theological persuasions may commune together within the same church, I would like to persuade the reader that credobaptist and credocommunion churches ought to sanction *the theological concept* of presumed regeneration and *the theological practices* of paedobaptism and paedocommunion. While it may seem novel and unpopular at first sight, I hope to show that this proposition is, at worst, a valid interpretation and, at best, the most likely interpretation of the Scriptures. If I am able to convince the reader of this then we will have a broad foundation upon which to rebuild the conservative evangelical church.

Church Defined

BEFORE ENTERING INTO THE particulars of why such a practice can and should be done, I must first start by clearly defining what I mean by *church*. Though there are numerous traditions within evangelicalism, the two poles between which there tends to be the most disagreement are the dispensational and covenantal theological systems. While each theory uses the terms *covenant* and *dispensation* within their own paradigm, these terms have come to be the defining marks that distinguish them. The difference between them should not be considered negligible, but they also should not reduce unity among evangelical Christian brothers. My hope in the ensuing paragraphs is to show why a primarily covenantal perspective on the Scriptures provides the foundation upon which this evangelical ecumenical movement could thrive and become a testimony to a divided world. Therefore, in order that this book might be protected from accusations of pretense, from the start I will lay out the covenantal perspective that drives my ecumenism. At the same time I hope to show that this theological framework allows for disagreement on non-fundamental issues within God's house.[1]

1. Defining *fundamental issues* will be dealt with later in this book under the heading "Conservative Evangelical Church Union."

Covenant Distinguished

In the third chapter of the apostle Paul's letter to the Ephesians we read a remarkable truth concerning the reason God commissioned him to preach the gospel to the gentile people. He writes in Eph 3:11, "This was according to the eternal purpose that he has realized in Christ Jesus our Lord." This singular noun translated as "purpose" may be understood as a combination of the prefix προ, meaning "before," and the root word τιθημι, which when functioning as a verb means "to place."[2] The phrase following explains how this singular "prior setting in place" was consummated in the person and the works of Jesus Christ. In the beginning of this epistle, Eph 1:4–14 introduces the apostle Paul's desire to credit the believers' inheritance to the predestination of God, which was according to his aforementioned πρόθεσιν. There are a number of observations that can be made from these verses, but I have chosen to highlight a particular principle—namely, that God the Father has *one* singular eternal purpose to bless his elect people with salvation through Jesus Christ. And notice that this verse says that it *has been* realized.[3]

The question then turns to how God accomplished this consummative purpose. In other words, how does God display his singular eternal πρόθεσιν? He does this through the two-sided coin of salvation—one side being individual election, the other side being corporate covenants. One side of the coin attends to his sovereign election of individuals, predestining them to salvation on the basis of his mere good pleasure (ευδοχία).[4] The other side of the coin is his corporate election of a people through the means of historical covenants, through which he works his special individual election. Thus, God accomplishes his eternal purposes by special (individual) election *and* general (corporate) election. While the two terms ought to remain unified in function they ought to be distinguished in manifestation. In order to appropriately answer

---

2. Brannan, *Lexham Analytical Lexicon.*

3. An aorist aspect that denotes summary or completion.

4. Brannan, *Lexham Analytical Lexicon.*

how God accomplishes his purpose, election and covenant must be kept together yet distinct. The one is invisible, the other visible. The one eternal, the other historical. The one presumed, the other known. The one subjective, the other objective. While the eternal election of God can in no way be infallibly known but only presumed on the basis of charity, "the covenant is God's administration of salvation in space and time, the historical outworking of his eternal plan."[5] As such, it may be known who is within the corporate elect—the church. Therefore, while there is a continuity between God's visible historical covenants and his invisible eternal election, there are also distinctions that must be made.

Because God eternally elects individuals *through* corporate historical covenants, there can be certainty that there are some within the covenant who are eternally elect. This is why much of Scripture speaks to the covenant people of God as if they are eternally elect even though some may not be. This is also why pastors can assure the congregation that God loves them even though some of these members might not be specially elect. Therefore, while there can be certainty that there are *some* within the covenant who are specially elect, it would be improper to argue that *only* the eternally elect are in covenant with God. This is not only contrary to the testimony of Scripture but also the experiences of the church. There may be some that are within a visible historical covenant with God who are not eternally elect unto salvation by God.

Romans chapters 9–11 give clear testimony to this principle. Some of God's covenant people Israel failed to obtain what the elect obtained. Romans 9:4 tells us that the covenants, promises, and even Christ himself belonged to the Israelites and yet Rom 9:6 makes the crucial argument "not all who are descended from Israel are Israel." Later on in Rom 11:11–24 he uses a metaphor of a tree that symbolizes the salvation of the people of God. In this metaphor he tells us that some of God's corporate covenant people, Israel, were broken off from the tree of the elect in order that the gentiles might be grafted in. A further example of this can be found

5. Lusk, "Covenant and Election," para. 1.

3

in 1 Cor 10:1–5 in which the apostle Paul declares that the people of Israel who were brought through the Red Sea by Moses truly did drink from the rock that was Christ, and yet God was not pleased with them. This shows that some of the Israelites were in a covenant with God, and yet were not eternally elect in Christ.[6]

A proper way to distinguish these different relationships between God and man is to call one a *covenantal union* and the other a *vital union*. That is, one can be regarded covenantally and corporately united with God while participating in the ordinances by which communion with God is possible, without actually being decretally and individually united in vital communion with God through persevering faith. Or, to paraphrase Rom 9:6, "not all those who appear to possess faith actually possess faith."

Covenant Defined

In his work *The Christ of the Covenants*, Palmer Robertson defines covenant as "a bond in blood sovereignly administered."[7] That is, a covenant can be defined as an oath with attached blessings for faithfulness and attached curses for unfaithfulness. Similar to the marriage covenant, a covenant simply commits people to each other. A simplified summary of Robertson's covenantal theology shows that God's relationship with his people can be divided into two archetypal covenants that endure for all time and find their consummation in Jesus Christ. The first is the *covenant of creation* that was inaugurated in Gen 1:28—2:17 between God and the first Adam. After the first Adam broke this covenant of creation, God was pleased to bind himself to man and ultimately fulfill the covenant of creation through the *covenant of redemption* beginning in Gen 3:15, which found its fulfillment in the person and works of Jesus Christ, the second Adam (Rom 5:12–21).[8] Through his perfect

---

6. Another example of this can be seen in Jude 1:5.

7. Robertson, *Christ of the Covenants*, 4.

8. Not to be confused with the classic Reformed label given by the Westminster Standards to a covenant between the members of the Trinitarian Godhead. See Robertson, *Christ of the Covenants*, 54.

life and atoning death Jesus restored the relationship between God and his people by fulfilling both the covenant of creation and redemption. So, whereas the covenant of creation created the man, the covenant of redemption *re*created the man.

In order to further substantiate this unity and distinction between covenant and election I would like to highlight the necessary components of a covenant found in those that God made under the covenant of creation with Adam and those that God made under the covenant of redemption with Adam, Noah, Abraham, Moses, David, and Christ.[9]

All Covenants Gracious

All covenants between God and man are an act of God's grace. God was not under any compulsion to create Adam nor to enter into a covenant with him, but he did exactly that because he is a gracious God. Further he could have destroyed Adam subsequent to his eating from the tree, but instead he graciously established the covenant of redemption. Noah found grace in the eyes of the Lord and so was honored with a covenant. When God sovereignly called Abraham to go from his homeland in order to receive a blessing, it was an act of grace. When he descended in a cloud on Mount Sinai to inscribe the Ten Commandments with his own finger, he did so in grace. When he chose the lowly shepherd boy David from the midst of his older, stronger brothers, he did so in grace. Thus, any covenant that is established between God and man has grace as its foundation. This is why Robertson would call a covenant "a bond in blood *sovereignly administered.*"[10] Covenants between God and man are always graciously initiated by God as sovereign and man as subject. In his critique of the classical Reformed designation of a *covenant of works* versus a *covenant of grace*, Robertson says, "To speak of a covenant

---

9. For a more in-depth study into these covenants, read Robertson, *Christ of the Covenants.*

10. Emphasis mine.

of 'works' in contrast with a covenant of 'grace' appears to suggest that grace was not operative in the covenant of works."[11]

This notion of all covenants being gracious also helps with the man-made division between law and gospel. While the gospel and law have different emphases, it must be noted that there is grace in the giving of God's commands. The apostle Paul cites the commandments given by Moses in Deut 30:14 when defending the doctrine of faith in Rom 10:5–8. The law in Moses was never meant to function separately from the promise and grace of God. Paul makes this explicit in Gal 3:17 where he tells us that the covenant of Moses did not abrogate the covenant of promise made with Abraham. God's covenant people do not spurn the law, but in recognizing that they are justified by grace they uphold the law knowing that it does not contradict grace but rather is empowered by grace. Therefore, the law and gospel are not in contradiction, but rather must be seen as two different manifestations of God's grace toward humanity. Without God's grace in the giving of the law the world would have no moral compass and would be left without any preserving graces, each man deciding what is right in his own eyes. Further, without the giving of the law man would not know his own sin.

This is why we must see all the covenants between God and man since the creation of the world as being a gracious condescension of God toward man, which progressively build upon each other in different dispensations and ultimately find their fulfillment in the person and the works of Jesus Christ.

All Covenants Conditional

All covenants have conditions that must be satisfied in order to receive the attached blessings. If these conditions are broken, there are consequences annexed to the breaking of the covenant. This is why Robertson helpfully calls a covenant "a *bond in blood* sovereignly

---

11. Robertson, *Christ of the Covenants*, 56.

administered."[12] Through his exhaustive study on the Hebrew word
כרת, meaning "to cut," Robertson shows that the concept of blood
is intimately associated with the inauguration of covenants.[13] The
covenants are inaugurated in blood in order to show the curses
that would be brought upon the offending party who breaks the
covenant.[14] The basic sentiment is this: "Let my blood be shed like
this animal if I were to be unfaithful to this covenant."

Even the new covenant is not without condition for the
church. The new covenant obligation to be counted among God's
people is clearly designated as faith in the death, burial, resurrection, and ascension of Jesus Christ. In order to apprehend the
atoning work done through his perfect life and substitutionary
death a person must have faith. To be sure, this faith is not a merit for justification just as no other works of righteousness merit
justification, but faith is the *instrument* of justification. In that
sense John Frame concludes, "Faith is an obligation, and in that
respect the command to believe is like other divine commands.
So it is impossible to say that a command, or law, is excluded
from the message of the gospel of grace."[15] All conditions for all
the covenants made between God and man have been satisfied
in the person and works of Jesus Christ, but they must be appre-
hended by faith. And while God gives the faith that he requires,
it is nonetheless a condition for justification. Thus, even the new
covenant church is not without her conditions.

While all covenants are gracious it is to be remembered that
all covenants have conditions annexed to them. No covenant

12. Emphasis mine.

13. "To cut" a covenant is found in Gen 15:18; 21:27; 26:28; 31:44; Exod
23:32, 34; 24:8; 34:10, 12, 15, 17; Deut 4:23; 5:2, 3; 7:2; 9:9; 29:1, 12, 14, 25,
29; 31:16; Josh 9:6; 24:25; Judg 2:2; 1 Sam 11:1, 2; 2 Sam 3:12; 1 Kgs 5:12; 2
Kgs 7:15; Isa 28:15; 55:3; Jer 11:10; 31:31; Ezek 17:13; Hos 2:18; Hag 2:5; Zech
11:10; Job 31:1; Ps 50:5; 1 Chr 11:3; 2 Chr 6:11; Ezra 10:3; Neh 9:8.

14. Gen 3:21(Adam), 9:5–6 (Noah), 15:9 (Abraham); Exod 24:8 (Moses);
the Davidic covenant does not expressly evidence blood in the making of the
covenant but does use the same verbiage, "to cut," as shown in the scriptures
above; Matt 26:28 (Christ).

15. Frame, *Doctrine of the Christian Life*, 187.

between two parties is ever established without conditions annexed to them that must be fulfilled in order to experience the full blessings of that particular covenant.

All Covenants Federal

All covenants require a representative head. That is, every covenant between God and man is established through the means of a mediator who acts as the head of the corporate entity of the people to whom God covenants himself. This federal head is then given the covenant and told to uphold the covenant for his own blessing *and* the blessing of his offspring. This normative principle of federal headship is seen throughout the Old Testament in that the children were considered a part of the covenant people of God because of their connection with their representative head—their father.[16] The burden of proof lies upon those who would claim that the new covenant implicitly requires the cessation of this federal headship ethic already present in the Old Testament Scriptures. Nowhere is there a restriction from baptism or the Lord's Supper laid upon the children of believing parents in the New Testament. This is troublesome for those who would argue otherwise, especially when considering the explicit exhortations to accept children as a part of the visible covenant people of God in passages such as Acts 2:39, 1 Cor 7:14, Rom 5:12–21, and Matt 19:14. This concept will be visited later.

All Covenants Signified

Seeing that covenants are the visible manifestation of God's eternal purpose, it makes sense that each covenant would be given a visible sign in order to assure the people that they are in proper covenant standing with their God. The extrabiblical

---

16. Gen 3:15; 9:9; 12:7; 13:15, 16; 15:18; 17:7–10, 19; 22:18; 24:7; 26:4–5; 35:12; 48:4; Num 18:19; Deut 4:37; 10:15; 30:6, 19; 2 Sam 7:12; 22:51; Esth 9:27; Pss 18:50; 25:13; 69:36; 89:4, 29, 36; 102:28; Prov 11:21; Isa 44:3; 45:25; 59:21.

Latin word *sacramentum* (sacrament) is the classic label given to these significations throughout the history of the church. *Sacramentum* is first used among the Alexandrian fathers and Tertullian.[17] In its classic usage, "sacramentum meant an oath, especially the oath taken by the military, and thus could refer to a solemn obligation."[18] Augustine rightfully divided the sacrament itself from the power of the sacrament.[19] In other words he saw the sign and the thing signified as separate concepts. Augustine defined this concept by saying that signs are called sacraments "because of their pertaining to divine things."[20]

Regardless, whether one calls it an ordinance or sacrament makes little difference. Both refer to the signs God has commanded his people to perform in order to signify and seal the covenant. Under the covenant of creation with Adam the sacrament was the tree of life, marriage, labor, and the Sabbath.[21] Under the covenant of redemption with Adam the sacrament was the animal skins. With Noah it was the bow in the clouds. With Abraham it was circumcision.[22] With Moses it was the tabernacle, the stone tablets of testimony, and the Sabbath. With David it was the throne. And with Christ's church under the new covenant it is baptism and the Lord's Supper.

To further strengthen the distinction between covenant and election I must reiterate that participation in the visible signs of the corporate covenant (the ordinances and sacraments) does not guarantee inclusion as a member of the individually specially elect of God. This is in strong contrast to the extreme sacramental theology that considers those who partake of the sacraments as the specially elect of God. While we ought to *presume* that those partaking in the signs of the covenant are elect, no sacrament has the ability

17. Kelly, *Early Christian Doctrines*, 193.

18. Ferguson, "Sacraments in the Pre-Nicene Period," 158.

19. Kelly, *Early Christian Doctrines*, 422.

20. Augustine, "Letter 138," ch. 1, para. 7.

21. Calvin, *Sermons on Genesis*, 339–43. Robertson would disagree and label the signs of the covenant of creation as marriage, the Sabbath, and labor.

22. Chapell, "Pastoral Overview of Infant Baptism," 12.

to infuse righteousness *ex opere operato*.[23] The sign and the thing signified in the ordinances flow out of the idea that the covenant is the visible manifestation of God's grace that signifies and seals the invisible eternal decree of God that is unknown. Therefore, one can participate in the corporate covenant ordinances without being individually and specially elected by God.

With the criteria for labeling the church shown above, it could be said that *the church is the visible corporate entity within God's covenant of redemption that has been given certain ordinances to signify and seal her special relationship with God.*

---

23. Translated from the Latin as "from the work performed."

History of Church Ordinances

Old Testament

WITH THE DEFINITION OF church behind us, we now turn to discussing the administration of the covenant ordinances. Within the old covenant, children are seen partaking in many of the covenant ordinances and were recipients of the covenant blessings. Consider the covenant ordinance of circumcision that was given by Abraham to his child. Consider the ordinance of the Passover feast in which children participated.[1] In Joel 2:16 we see the explicit inclusion of nursing infants within the congregation of Israel who were to be consecrated. Consider the children who participated in the sacrificial meals of Lev 10:14 and Num 18:11. The Old Testament shows that the people of God presumed that their children were well established within the covenant without having to confess the tenets of the faith. Rayburn defends the inclusion of children from their youngest days in the old covenant ordinances by saying, "At no point do we encounter as we might expect . . . a covenant child being prepared for or granted entrance into this sacramental participation, having reached a certain age

---

1. Keidel, "Is the Lord's Supper for Children?" 307–8. Keidel has done a masterful job arguing for the inclusion of infants at the Passover feast on the basis of connecting the phrase "each one according to the mouth of his eating" in Deut 12:4 with Deut 16:16–21. In doing this he shows that just as the children were included in eating the manna in the wilderness by this phrase, so, too, they were included in the Passover meal.

or having crossed some spiritual boundary."[2] While some might argue that this old covenant participation was purely predicated on physical descent, the Scriptures reveal a dual requirement for participation in the covenant people of God even under the old covenant dispensation; one requirement was physical while the other was presumed faith and repentance in God.[3] Consider Rom 4:11, which attaches the spiritual and physical reality into one saying that Abraham "received the sign of circumcision *as a seal* of the righteousness that he had by faith while he was still uncircumcised."[4] Circumcision was a seal of a previously presumed faith. Even in the old covenant presumption of faith preceded admittance to the ordinances of the covenant. But again, even though an infant was included in the visible covenant people of God and participated in the ordinances of the people of God, it did not *guarantee* that infant's right to the invisible telic reward of salvation through the long awaited Messiah Jesus Christ.

Pre-Nicene

Leaving the New Testament proof texts for later, the history of the church under the new covenant reveals a broad and consistent inclusion of infants in the covenant people of God. While the history of the church is filled with flaws in judgment, there has been a consistent thread of orthodoxy practiced throughout her history. I would like to follow the often complicated flow of new covenant sacramentality (the administration of the ordinances) from the pre-Nicene era of the church (prior to the Council of Nicaea in 325) to the post–Great Awakening era of the church (after the seventeenth- and eighteenth-century Puritanism and revivalism).

In the earliest days of the church much was being practiced without a full-fledged understanding of why it was being done.

2. Rayburn, "Presbyterian Defense of Paedocommunion," 7.

3. Isa 1:10–20; Lev 23:27–29; Ps 51:16–19; Exod 12:48.

4. Emphasis mine.

As you might expect, some of these practices were based on incorrect understandings of Scripture while most were done with an orthodox understanding of Scripture. During this period the vast array of church fathers believed that baptism washed away original sin and that it was necessary to lead a sinless life after baptism.[5] Hence, the reason some waited many years, even until their deathbed, to be baptized was for the expressed purpose that more sins might be washed away.

The normative mode of baptism from the earliest days of the church was either full body immersion or standing waist deep in water with water poured over the head.[6] Some of the credobaptist persuasion might think to capitalize on these modes of baptism claiming that infants most certainly could not have been subjects of these immersive types of baptism, but this is not the case. Consider how, even to this day, the Greek church practices the immersion of infants during their baptism.

Origen along with Hippolytus explicitly make mention of the practice of infant baptism stretching back to the time of the apostles.[7] Within *The Apostolic Tradition* Hippolytus recommends the order of baptisms as follows, "First the little ones should be baptized. All who can speak for themselves should speak. For those however who cannot, their parents or another who belongs to their family should speak."[8]

Some correctly point out that Tertullian was hesitant to baptize infants but incorrectly conclude that infant baptism was an invention of his time. This anecdote gives unintended assistance to the paedobaptist faction by showing that this practice of infant baptism was a well established practice in North Africa against which Tertullian was arguing as a minority. It also fails to show the

5. Stander and Louw, *Baptism*, 38.

6. Ferguson, *Baptism*, 857. Ferguson provides the supreme historical assessment of not only the early church's understanding of baptism, but of the Jewish community's understanding of baptismal cleansing through the mode of full immersion.

7. Jeremias, *Infant Baptism*, 66.

8 Bradshaw et al., *Apostolic Tradition*, 95.

contextual nuances of his argument. Rather than arguing against baptizing infants of believing parents, which he commends in his later writings,[9] Tertullian recommended that the adult *pagan* converts along with their children hesitate before baptism in order that they might not rush into a commitment they could not actually fulfill.[10] Furthermore, Tertullian's sacramental beliefs might be shown in his influence upon Cyprian of Carthage. Cyprian's writings during the early 250s expressed not only an endorsement of infant baptism but also of infant communion.[11]

So while the theology of this era may have been immature, in that some gave mystical *ex opere operato* powers of the ordinances of baptism and the Lord's Supper, it is clear that the standard in the early church was to include infants of believing parents in the visible covenant body of the church. This inclusion granted them the right to partake in the ordinances contained therein. Leithart correctly concludes, "Infant baptism was the rule long before there was much of a coherent theology to explain why it was done."[12]

Post-Nicene and Medieval

Augustine of Hippo stands out as the chief torch bearer of orthodoxy between the times of the pre-Nicene era and the Reformation. His understanding of infant baptism was developed in the midst of the Pelagian controversy. Pelagius recognized infants as pure and sinless at birth, but Augustine fought vigorously against this in order to hold fast to the doctrine of total depravity in the unregenerate infant. He sought to provide a basis for the cleansing of this depravity from each of the infants through baptism. "For from the infant newly born to the old man bent with age,

---

9. In *De Anima* 39:3—40:1, Tertullian expounds on 1 Cor 7:14 by arguing, "The children of a mixed marriage are holy, both because of their descent from a Christian parent and also because of their future education in Christian doctrine." Tertullian, *De Anima*, 220.

10. Jeremias, *Infant Baptism*, 82.

11. Cyprian, *Epistles*, 444.

12. Leithart, "Infant Baptism," 251.

as there is none shut out from baptism, so there is none who in baptism does not die to sin. But infants die only to original sin."[13] It is easy to see that his doctrine of baptism, for better or for worse, was intricately linked with his assessment of the total depravity of man. Though Augustine was somewhat deficient as to a nuanced covenantal understanding of baptism, his sacramental theology supported the orthodox understanding of a salvation absolutely predicated on the grace of God. No one in the early church prior to him more clearly "recognized the radical helplessness of man or the radical necessity of being born again into Christ."[14]

When Augustine spoke of the ordinances, and in particular the Lord's Supper, he did so by using the terms *sacramentum* and *res*—the sign and the thing signified. Due to this distinction, Augustine did not believe that the sacrament of the Lord's Supper infused grace but rather conveyed it. The Lord's Supper pointed to the substance of the redemption found only in Christ.[15] Because of this he did not exclude from the Supper those who were unable to express faith in a verbal or clearly manifest way. Rather he included baptized infants in the Lord's Supper saying, "Yes, they are infants, but they are his members. They are infants, but they receive his sacraments."[16] Further, while substantiating his argument against the Donatists of the time who refused to allow apostates back into the church, Augustine argued that the church is a mixed body of both sinners and saints. This showed that Augustine considered that there are some within the church who partake of the sacraments of baptism and the Lord's Supper and yet are not elected unto salvation.[17]

After Augustine the church was met with an age of mysticism and scholasticism in which the doctrine of transubstantiation reared its Platonistic head. This doctrine plagued the understanding of who was to be considered within the covenant of the church

---

13. Augustine, *Enchiridion*, 252.

14. Leithart, "Infant Baptism," 260.

15. Fitzgerald, *Augustine Through the Ages*, 334.

16. Augustine, *Sermons*, 261.

17. Kelly, *Early Christian Doctrines*, 416.

and thus to receive the Lord's Supper. Rather than a sacramental view of the bread and wine, much of the church was fooled to believe the bread and the wine were the actual substantial body and blood of the risen and ascended Jesus. Because of this there was much focus on not profaning the body and blood of Jesus. It was around this time that the doctrine of transubstantiation was codified during the Fourth Lateran council in 1215. Upon this codification people began to question just who could worthily receive the body and blood of Jesus without profaning it. They began to wonder if infants or other sick people in the congregation might profane the Lord by not swallowing the elements properly and as a result spit or vomit them out.[18] And so the tradition of bringing young children to the table was lost due to the medieval doctrine of transubstantiation. This did not go unchallenged as the Hussites led by Jan Hus and Jakoubek of Stribo in Bohemia sought to restore both the laity and the infant to the table of the Lord's Supper. Again we are led to see that infants of believing parents were included in both the ordinances of the church in many areas of Christendom in the post-Nicene and medieval era.

Reformation

While the doctrine of transubstantiation was vigorously attacked by the Reformers, its chief outworking of barring covenantal infants from the table was yet retained. Thus, broadly speaking infants were barred from the Lord's Supper until reaching an age where they were able to confess and explicitly manifest some manner of Christian faith. Happily they were not barred from the waters of baptism. Quite the contrary, the Reformation gladly received into membership of the church those infants of believing parents.

Luther believed baptized infants gained their vital union with Christ through the waters of baptism and could lose it through apostasy, and so argued for the importance (some Lutheran

18. Nicoletti, "History of Credocommunion," 28.

historians might argue necessity) of baptizing infants. While it might seem on the surface that Luther advocated for a justification through baptism *ex opere operato*, the following from Luther makes clear otherwise: "Baptism justifies nobody, and gives advantage to nobody; rather, faith in the word of the promise to which baptism was conjoined, is what justifies, and so completes, that which the baptism signified."[19] In his baptism of infants, even his doctrine of vital baptismal regeneration, Luther argues for the orthodox calling card of salvation by grace through faith. The faith of the infant was upon the waters of baptism and conjoined with it.

His French contemporary John Calvin also exhorted and demanded the inclusion of covenantal children into the waters of baptism. Calvin argued that even before the baptism of the covenant child that God was already at work. In what can rightly be classified as Calvin's concept of *presumed* regeneration he says, "They are already of the flock of Christ, of the family of God, since the covenant of salvation which God enters into with believers is common also to their children. . . . In one word, unless we choose to overturn all the principles of religion, we shall be obliged to confess that the salvation of an infant does not depend on, but is only *sealed* by its baptism."[20] In his *Acts of the Council of Trent with the Antidote* he argues once again for the presumption of the covenant child's holiness and thus their right to the waters of baptism by using 1 Cor 7:14: "Nay, on what ground do we admit them to baptism unless that they are the heirs of promise?"[21] This understanding of baptism undergirded the Reformed principle that salvation rests not on any particular knowledge or experience or self-proclaimed decision of our own, but entirely upon the grace of God that was given to believers and also presumed to be given to their offspring.

After Luther, Calvin, and other early Reformers, this distinction between the covenant people of God and the elect people of God began to be lost during the Arminian controversy. The

---

19. Luther, *Word and Sacrament II*, 59–60.

20. Calvin, *1554–1558*, 279; emphasis added.

21. Calvin, *Acts of the Council of Trent*, sec. "On the Sixth Session," para. 3.

Reformed churches became enveloped in the theology of the invisibly elect in order to resist the Roman Catholic–leaning influence of Jacobus Arminius and his proponents, and so the theology of the visible covenant people of God was subtly subsumed into the concept of the invisibly elect.

Other later Reformers maintained some measure of nuanced distinction between election and covenant. Turretin shows a "seed principle" of regeneration by which infants of believers were said to be members of the covenant: "Infants . . . can be capacious of passive regeneration, as to the principle and the impression of the divine image, which ought to exert itself in its own time. . . . If it was right for infants to be brought to Christ [Matt 19:14], why not also to be received to baptism, the symbol of our communion with Christ? Why should the church not receive into her bosom those whom Christ received into his?. . . Because the children of believers are holy [1 Cor 7:14]; therefore they ought to be baptized . . . they are said to be holy by a federal holiness."[22] And Hermann Witsius gives an even clearer understanding of the distinction between vital inward regeneration and the covenantal external regeneration when he says, "God has given that pledge to pious parents that they may *regard* their little ones as the children of God by gracious adoption, until, when further advanced, they betray themselves by indications to the contrary, and that they may feel not less secure regarding their children dying in infancy than did Abraham and Isaac of old."[23] Again, even though covenant children were sadly withheld from the Lord's Table we see that covenant inclusion of infants was broadly seen in the church's administration of baptism during the era of the Reformation.

Post–Great Awakenings

Covenant theology took a metaphysical and experiential punch during the seventeenth- and eighteenth-century era of the Great

22. Turretin, *Institutes*, 3:417–19.
23. Witsius, "Efficacy and Utility of Baptism," 128; emphasis added.

Awakening brought on by Puritanism and revivalism. As a result of careless practice of some Reformed pastors and churches, baptism was frequently given to infants "irrespective of faith on the part of the parents."[24] Many pushed back against the formalism that had so largely supplanted true religion and experience, and this movement became known as the Great Awakening.[25] This is another classic case of a pendulum swinging too far to one side only to swing back to the extreme on the other. Experience began to outpace the theology that should have supported it. The extraordinary means of conscious conversion experiences supplanted the ordinary means of word and sacrament within the life of the church. Nurture of childlike faith from one's youth was replaced by an expectation for an experiential mature faith. With an eager desire to show the vitality of their faith, many Christians disparaged traditional interpretations of the Scripture, liturgy within the church, and ecclesial leadership. During the Second Great Awakening in America, "ordinary men and women increasingly failed to take into account the standard theological guides that served as guides for religious experience."[26] As my Baptist pastor put it, "Rather than letting the Scriptures interpret the experience, some allow experience to interpret the Scriptures."[27] This reality was all too common during the period of the Great Awakenings. Though many of the doctrines taught by the great evangelists and leaders of the Great Awakenings were the doctrines that in large part aligned with the Magisterial Reformers, they strayed in some teachings by catering to individual experientialism over and against a proper theological framework. In their reaction against the formalism of many so-called Reformed

24. Schenck, *Presbyterian Doctrine*, 53.

25. Schenck, *Presbyterian Doctrine*, 53–57. Puritan Samuel Rutherford rightly saw the church as the institution of salvation, but improperly applied this principle, even advocating for the enforcement of presumably unregenerate men into membership.

26. Hatch, *Democratization*, 34.

27. Pastor Drew Fenstermacher has been largely influential on this work due to his brotherly nature despite doctrinal differences. This was one of his many wise sayings that has informed my hermeneutic.

churches, these revivalist preachers asserted only one means by which to recognize the true children of God—experience.[28]

Consequently, the presumption that infants of believing parents were within the covenant people of God was soon excluded on the grounds that infants could not evidence a certain invisible inward experience with God. In what became known as the Halfway Covenant, Presbyterian ministers began to reel from the historic Reformed conclusion that children of believers were presumably regenerated, instead positing that they are presumably unregenerated and therefore only brought into the visible covenant people of God through baptism, denying a prior inward regeneration. As it went, "Until by conscious conversion children of the covenant came out of the darkness and evil of despair . . . all recognition of their standing in the sight of God as His children was lost."[29] Rather than assuming that God had a special watchful eye for his covenant children to whom he promised to be God, many preachers during the Great Awakening, like Cotton Mather, considered covenant children as "the wild ass's colt."[30] It is very unfortunate that the Great Awakening, which was largely grounded in Reformation theology, in no small way directed their attack not only against the lukewarm members of the church but also against all children within the church. Trouwborst argues that this treatment of covenant children was already codified in some Puritan theology: "Well before the First Great Awakening, the model of conversion experience replaced the pattern of covenant succession and in some measure established the need for such an ideal, dramatic conversion event."[31] Fearful little children wandering about fretting about whether they had been "convicted enough," or if they prayed the prayer the right way, or whether they were truly converted unto Christ. "It was taken for granted that children must, or in all ordinary cases would, grow up unconverted."[32] Speaking

28. Hatch, *Democratization*, 64.
29. Hatch, *Democratization*, 67.
30. Mather, *Family Well-Ordered*, 6.
31. Trouwborst, "Covenant to Chaos," 101.
32. Schenck, *Presbyterian Doctrine*, 71.

of this conversion ethic one replied, "Everyone's religious experience must be broken up into the prescribed measure and form. . . . Everyone must believe certain things, and do certain things, and pass through a certain process, or he is lost."[33]

Devalued in all of this was the exhortation to confidently gaze toward the person and the works of Christ. Instead of looking to the experiences of Christ they were directed to their own experiences. While the Great Awakenings served as a somewhat helpful corrective to nominalism that was seeping into undisciplined churches that practiced infant baptism, it was not capable of being a perpetual standard for ecclesial praxis. As Charles Hodge rightly noted about the Great Awakening,

> It may be highly useful, or even necessary, just as violent remedies are often the only means of saving life. But such remedies are not the ordinary and proper means of sustaining and promoting health. . . . No one can fail to remark that this too exclusive dependance on revivals tends to produce a false or unscriptural form of religion. . . . The ordinary means of grace become insipid or distasteful. . . . Perhaps however the most deplorable result of the mistake we are now considering is, the neglect which it necessarily induces of the divinely appointed means of careful Christian nurture. . . . Family training of children, and pastoral instruction of the young, are almost entirely lost sight of. We have long felt and often expressed the conviction that this is one of the most serious evils in the present state of our churches.[34]

While some measure of a vital experiential union with God is to be desired, this can only come by gazing upon Jesus Christ and his experiences, not by relying upon our own. Thus, this impression that one needed to have a vivid conversion experience or to remember a time when they said a prayer is a key pivot point in what soon became the American Baptist model for exclusive church membership and baptism.

---

33. Dewey, *Letters of an English Traveler*, 120–21.
34. Hodge, "Review," 520–21.

Recipients of the Church Ordinances

Defining Regeneration

IN CONTRAST TO THE experientialism that so pervades our post-modern culture, there has been a renewal of the classic Reformed distinction between the concepts of covenantal union and vital union, and thus a renewal of who ought to be considered the recipient of baptism and church membership. This renewal was in large part restored to its rightful place by Old Princeton Theology and the Dutch Reformed.[1] Take, for instance, this extended stance of B. B. Warfield in his effort to restore a proper understanding of covenant succession and the restoration of infants of believing parents to the waters of baptism:

> If we say that [the church's] attitude should be as exclusive as possible, and that it must receive as the children of Christ only those whom it is forced to recognize as such, then we shall inevitably narrow the circle of the subjects of baptism to the lowest limits. If, on the other hand, we say that its attitude should be as inclusive as possible, and that it should receive as the children of Christ all whom, *in the judgment of charity*, it may fairly recognize as such, then we shall naturally widen the circle of the subjects of baptism to far more ample limits. The former represents, broadly speaking, the Puritan idea of the Church, the

1. Trouwborst, "Covenant to Chaos," 89.

latter the general Protestant doctrine. It is on the basis of the Puritan conception of the Church that the Baptists are led to exclude infants from baptism. For, if we are to demand anything like demonstrative evidence of actual participation in Christ before we baptize, no infant, who by reason of years is incapable of affording signs of his union with Christ, can be thought a proper subject of the rite. The vice of this system, however, is that it attempts the impossible. No man can read the heart. As a consequence, it follows that no one, however rich his manifestation of Christian graces, is baptized on the basis of infallible knowledge of his relation to Christ. All baptism is inevitably administered on the basis not of knowledge but of presumption.[2]

Warfield argued against the conception of a pristine church that had no tares mixed with wheat. His argument for presumed regeneration was that all regeneration is presumed and the ability to infallibly know the heart of a person is not the job of the church. As Schenck notes, "God had not given to man the power to search the heart, he had not imposed upon them any duty which implied the possession of such a power. In other words, Christ had not committed to men the impossible task of making a church which consisted exclusively of the regenerate."[3]

At this point it would be proper to distinguish the term *regeneration*. Is regeneration a metaphysical change or a relational change? Does it deal with the eternal invisible election of God or the historical visible covenant of God? The classic Protestant understanding is that it deals with both. Regeneration has both a subjective metaphysical sense and an objective locative sense. Subjectively speaking, regeneration is the unchangeable secret inward work of the Holy Spirit. Objectively speaking, it is a matter of entering into a new life with new status as an adopted child in the visible covenant family of the church. Similar to the ordinances that are a sign of the thing signified, *ecclesial* regeneration (inclusion in the

2. Warfield, "Polemics of Infant Baptism," 389–90. Also see Hodge, "Church Membership of Infants," 351.

3. Schenck, *Presbyterian Doctrine*, 128.

church) is a sign of the presumed *internal* regeneration that takes place in the hearts of believers. This distinction between the two helps strengthen the Reformed understanding of the sign and the thing signified. The ecclesial regeneration, under which the child of a believer is passively brought into covenant union with God, is a strong sign of the passive nature of the internal regeneration that takes place in a person's soul by the power of the Holy Spirit. Calvin shows his agreement with this idea of ecclesial regeneration saying, "For as God, regenerating us in baptism, ingrafts us into the fellowship of his Church, and makes us his by adoption, so we have said that he performs the office of a provident parent, in continually supplying the food by which he may sustain and preserve us in the life to which he has begotten us by his word."[4] By this he does not deviate from his doctrine of justification by grace through faith, nor does he advocate for the Roman Catholic understanding of the infusion unto the soul by the waters of baptism. Rather he is simply conveying that we are engrafted into the church by baptism. This does not mean ecclesial regeneration is just an empty sign with no benefits, but rather that it does convey grace and *normatively* is congruent with a vital regeneration.

Hodge rightly points out that there are different definitions of regeneration that color its interpretation. While one definition of regeneration refers to the external change in which one is taken out of the world and placed into the external covenant people of God, the more common post–Synod of Dort (1618–19) definition is that which describes an internal spiritual renewal.[5] Prior to this instantaneous metaphysical focus, Calvin referred to regeneration as a lifelong process: "This restoration does not take place in one moment or one day or one year; but through continual and sometimes even slow advances God wipes out in his elect the corruptions of the flesh, cleanses them of guilt, consecrates them to himself as temples, renewing all their minds to true purity that they may practice repentance throughout their lives and know that this

4. Calvin, *Institutes* (Beveridge), 896.
5. Hodge, *Soteriology*, 591.

warfare will only end at death."[6] This has scriptural support in Matt 19:28 where Jesus speaks of regeneration in terms of a location rather than a one-time event. He tells his disciples that his followers will sit on thrones παλιγγενεσίᾳ (literally in the again birth).[7] Thus we can see that regeneration can be defined in an objective locative sense rather than only the subjective metaphysical sense. This particular usage of regeneration denotes the location of the church as the root for this "again birth." The church, in which the apostles will express judgment (i.e., sit upon thrones), is the center and the foundation for the renewal of creation, and thus to enter into her is to enter into the "again birth," objectively speaking.

Both the subjective and objective definitions of regeneration might be seen in Titus 3:5 where the apostle Paul says, "[God our Savior] saved us . . . by[/through] the washing of regeneration [παλιγγενεσίας] and renewal [ἀνακαινώσεως] of the Holy Spirit." The first sense of the word translated "regeneration" can be considered as the combination of παλιν, meaning "again," and γενεσίας, meaning "birth,"[8] thus it could be translated by the common evangelical idiom "born again." It is interesting to note that he describes this as the *washing* of regeneration, which properly conveys the Christian rite of baptism. This is that objective locative change that is done to a person when they enter into the covenant people of God. The second sense of the word *regeneration* in Titus 3:5 can be seen in that we are saved by/through the "renewal of the Holy Spirit." This is that subjective metaphysical change that is done on the soul of the believer through faith.

It is a reasonable interpretation to conclude that regeneration in this verse is described both in an external visible manner and an internal invisible manner. In other words, Paul might be teaching Titus during his church-planting initiative that the *normative way* a person is saved is through the entrance into the external covenant people by baptism *and* vitally through the inward work of the Holy Spirit. *Normatively*, the means of salvation for the elect are the Holy

---

6. Calvin, *Institutes* (Beveridge), 391.

7. Brannan, *Lexham Analytical Lexicon*.

8. Brannan, *Lexham Analytical Lexicon*.

Spirit *and* Christ's church. Obviously there are drastic exceptions to this, say if a person were to repent and place faith in Christ apart from being baptized or if a Christian child were to perish before they are baptized. These persons would be saved by the inward regeneration of the Holy Spirit without having experienced the external ecclesial "regeneration" of church inclusion. Titus 3:5 only describes the *normative* principle of salvation.

While this gives helpful nuance to the Reformed concept of regeneration I will argue that regeneration as it is used in the term *presumed regeneration* is that initial internal vital union wrought by the Holy Spirit. It might be added that we ought not separate regeneration and faith, just like we cannot separate life from breathing. Therefore, when I argue that we ought to presume that infants of believers are regenerated, I presume that that infant possesses faith. So then, because we presume the infant of believers to be *vitally* united with Christ on the basis of God's promises to be God to believers and their seed, we bring them into *covenantal* union with Christ through the waters of baptism and the elements of the Lord's Supper.

The Capacity for and Reality of Infant Faith

Now that we have distinguished regeneration, is there a scriptural basis to argue for presumed vital regeneration in the infant of believing parents? First, do infants have the capacity to possess faith? And second, what is the warrant to believe that children of believing parents actually do possess faith?

One exegetical point might be sustained in 2 Tim 3:15 where Paul exhorts Timothy to continue in what he has known (οἶδας) from his childhood (ἀπὸ βρέφους). This word translated as "childhood" is translated in other scriptures as "infant," "baby," or "young child."[9] Most notably this word is only used in the Gospel of Luke, who is considered to have written the Gospel on the basis of Paul's apostolic authority. Therefore on the basis that "Luke

---

9. Brannan, *Lexham Analytical Lexicon.*

alone" was with Paul during his writing of 2 Timothy (2 Tim 4:11), and assuming Luke himself wrote the letter of 2 Timothy on the basis of the apostle Paul's authority, we might gain more insight into Luke's usage of βρέφους in 2 Tim 3:15. In Luke 1:41 and 44, we see this same word used to describe the preborn John the Baptist leaping for joy in the womb of his mother upon the arrival of the expecting mother of Jesus. This understanding of the word shows that Luke considers the capacity for infants to express faith and possess the Holy Spirit. Luke 2:12, 16, and 18:15 show clearly Luke's intended usage of this word referring to infants. Therefore in returning to 2 Tim 3:15, it would be proper to hold that Paul presumed Timothy was vitally united to God as an infant because of his connection with his grandmother and mother's faith. Note that the verb οἶδας is in the perfect tense and describes a past action with a present result. So Paul believes Timothy's knowledge of the Lord extends backward to his infancy.

In arguing for the persistence in a marriage with an unbeliever the apostle Paul tells us in 1 Cor 7:14, "The unbelieving husband is made holy because of his wife, and the unbelieving wife is made holy because of her husband. Otherwise your children would be unclean, but as it is, they are holy." Rather than concluding that the children likewise *are made holy* (ἡγίασται) similar to the husband or wife, the text tells us that the children of the believing parent *are holy* (ἅγιά ἐστιν).[10] They are described as indicatively and statively holy. This can only show the apostle Paul's presumption that children are to be considered differently from unbelieving adults; that children are to be considered holy because of their natural connection with a believing parent.[11]

During his sermon at Pentecost, the apostle Peter directed his listeners who had been "pierced in heart" that they were to repent and be baptized, and that they would receive the gift of the Holy Spirit. He then declared that "the promise is for these listeners and their children" (Acts 2:39). This would have been a

---

10. Brannan, *Lexham Analytical Lexicon.*

11. Joachim Jeremias provides an in depth analysis of the language used here in 1 Cor 7 in his book *Infant Baptism in the First Four Centuries.*

natural assumption for Jews who lived under the old covenant dispensation, who considered their children as vitally united to God by giving them the *seal* of circumcision. This perpetual promise from Peter secured the idea that the children of believers were to continue to be considered as part of the community and those to whom the Holy Spirit was promised. Again, lineage from Christian parents does not certainly secure eternal election, but rather these covenant children are to be considered as part of the elect. The apostle Peter, speaking as one well acquainted with Old Testament federal headship and covenant sentiment, would need to give an explicit exclusion of these children of believing parents in order to warrant a groundbreaking change as pertains to covenant inclusion. But no explicit exclusion is seen in the text, and therefore the burden of proof is laid upon those who would exclude these children.

Another proof might be evidenced in 2 Sam 12:23 where, after David had interceded with the Lord on behalf of his child, he is told about the child's death. In response to the question posed to him about why he so quickly recouped his losses David responded, "Why should I fast? Can I bring him back again? I shall go to him, but he will not return to me." What is the ground for David's assurance that he will go to see the child if not for the belief that the child was regenerated and possessed faith?[12]

Perhaps a less explicit proof of the presumption of faith in the children of believers can be found in Eph 6:4 where Paul commands Christian fathers to raise up their children "in the discipline and instruction of the Lord." The genitival phrase "of the Lord" (κυρίου) can be seen as a subjective genitive since it is connected with two head nouns that have an implicit verbal idea (παιδεία and νουθεσία).[13] Because of this we ought to interpret this phrase as if the father is expressing the Lord's discipline upon the child. If this is the case, then the Lord would be disciplining the child as if it were one of his own. And from Heb 12:6, where this

---

12. Some reasonably argue that David intends that he will go to Sheol (he will die) rather than going to heaven.

13. Brannan, *Lexham Analytical Lexicon*.

infrequent word παιδεύω is used to quote Prov 3:11–12, we know that God only disciplines those whom he loves.[14] Thus, when Paul commands this to the fathers he is commanding them to consider their children as little Christians.

Along with the above passages, Pss 8:2, 22:9–10, 71:6, and Isa 46:3 show that nursing infants and even preborn infants of believing parents can and do possess faith.

The concept of capacity for infant faith is not alien to Baptist believers. Though they might draw a line at a slightly later age, they are still remarkably charitable in their perception of the young within the church. Even though they might not be baptized, all those who are born into the families of Baptist churches are functionally considered as a part of the "church family." Most of my Baptist brothers and sisters strive to catechize their children from a very young age. They teach them to pray "Our Father" when praying. They love to see their children singing "Father Abraham" or "Jesus Loves Me" at a young age.[15] They praise God upon hearing the innocent faith of a two year old who says, "I love Jesus." They pray with their children after disciplining them and assure them of the forgiveness that they have in Jesus. All of these actions and ones that are not mentioned are done with the assumption that a child is capacious to possess faith. Otherwise, they are simply lying to children and giving them false confidence. Baptists value children and consider them as one of their most precious gifts given to them by God. Seeing then that my Baptist brethren would agree that children are capable of glorifying God in their hearts, and seeing the exegetical evidence that is given for the capacity of faith in infants, this concept of presumed regeneration should not come as a stretch nor as an unacceptable doctrine to practice within a credobaptist church.

For those credobaptists that are not convinced by this exegetical and practical evidence, the burden of proof falls upon them to show that this presumption of regeneration in the children of believers did not take place within the covenant people

14. Brannan, *Lexham Analytical Lexicon*.
15. Warner, "Jesus Loves Me."

of God within the Scriptures. Additionally the burden of proof falls upon them to show that a profession of faith is needed before entering into the waters of baptism. If the argument is made that paedobaptism ought to be a restricted practice because there is no clear example of infants being baptized in the New Testament, then similarly women partaking in the Lord's Supper ought to be a restricted practice since there is no explicit example of them participating at the Lord's Table. But none of my Baptist brethren would ever deny a woman the Table.

Not to be outdone, many proponents of paedobaptism also have to deal with a burden of proof. While they allow infants to partake in the waters of baptism, they restrict access to the Lord's Table by requiring a profession of faith in order to become a "communing member" of the church. This is what can be known as credocommunion. Is this not the same rhetoric used by the Baptists as it pertains to baptism? At least the credobaptist faction has kept a consistent standard for participation in both ordinances of the church. Contrary to most Reformed Christians today, I would like to argue on the basis of Scripture that those who have faith and have received baptism ought to be invited to the Lord's table. Most Christians who would prohibit young children from participating in the Lord's Supper do so on the basis of 1 Cor 11:28, "Let a person examine himself, then, and so eat of the bread and drink of the cup." The rhetoric goes that since infants and young children do not have the wherewithal to examine themselves properly then they ought to be excluded from the Table. But in a similar manner, what ought to be done with the old saint who has faithfully served the church for decades only to be plagued by Alzheimer's that prohibits him from adequately "examining himself"? Should he be excluded from the Supper? Of course not!

As Jefferey Meyers effectively argues, the verse ought to be more appropriately translated, "Let a man *prove* himself and so eat of the bread and drink of the cup." This translation is based upon Paul's larger usage of the word δοκιμαζω used throughout the rest of the Pauline corpus.[16] Thus, "a man 'proves himself' by

---

16. Meyers, "Presbyterian, Examine Thyself," 21.

how he eats, not how much he understands or how thoroughly he searches his heart."[17] This is further expounded by verse 29 when he elaborates that condemnation falls on those who do not consider "the body." Within the larger context of 1 Cor it is much more appropriate to consider "the body" being spoken of here as the church. Many were not treating their brothers and sisters well and thus were dividing the church while eating the Lord's Supper. Paul condemned this and made it a prerequisite that any baptized member who participates at the Lord's Table ought to be in good standing within the church, not causing division. Seeing that a baptized infant or young child normally does not have this power to divide the church in the ways shown in this epistle, they should in no way be barred from the Lord's Supper.

This falls in line with the historic church's understanding of *excommunication* (i.e., barring from the Supper) on the basis of one's explicit divisive and disobedient behavior. Excommunication was done by ordained clergy of the church on the basis of objective disqualifications, not by laymen upon their own subjective self-examination. Therefore, members of the church ought not excommunicate themselves from the Supper based on some internal subjective judgment of their spiritual standing with God, but rather should depend upon the proper ordained authorities to judge whether they have been a member in good standing within the church body. If there is no objective explicit division caused by a person, then they ought to be allowed to participate in the Lord's Supper. If they are "considering the body," then they ought to partake. So, if we presume that children of believers possess faith and so rightfully give them baptism, we also ought to include them at the Lord's Table when they are prepared to eat on their own accord. Likewise we ought not to bar the old saint with Alzheimer's from the Table on the basis that he cannot examine himself.

Children of believers are capable of and really do possess faith. If any were to deny it, why would our Lord graciously invite them to his side and use them as the representatives for all citizens of heaven? (Matt 19:14, Mark 10:14, Luke 18:16). It is a dangerous precedent to

17. Meyers, "Presbyterian, Examine Thyself," 21.

restrict children from coming to Jesus through participation with him in his death, burial, and resurrection in the waters of baptism and the elements of the Lord's Supper. This goes against the very imperative of Jesus to "ἄφετε τὰ παιδία ἔρχεσθαι πρός με" (Leave the children to come to me)!

A Charitable Mediating Ethic—Presumed Regeneration

This doctrine of presumed regeneration can be a powerful mediating ethic between increasingly separated paedo and credo believers. While some might react strongly to the verbiage of presumed regeneration, it is consistent with the practice of the historic church. If presumed regeneration is too striking, perhaps Bavinck's conclusion would provide a reprieve from the shock. He preferred to say that Reformed theologians always held that such regeneration in infancy can occur, often does occur, and that the church is to *consider* and *treat* her children, according to the judgment of love, not as heathen children but as true children of the covenant until they prove the contrary. While the difference between presumption of regeneration and the opinion of Bavinck is small, I would gladly give way to the nomenclature if the practice of covenant succession were implemented in the church.[18] Regardless, those in the Reformed camp like myself who presume regeneration in the infants of believers and who desire to give them the ordinance of baptism do so on the presupposition that only those who are presumed to possess faith ought to be admitted to baptism and church membership. Baptism is the seal of a *previous* faith. This is the same standard used by Baptists. While most Baptists require a profession of faith as the standard for whether one is able to receive baptism or not, most would not absolutely require profession in cases where it is impossible. Consider, for instance, the examples of the mute, the mentally incapacitated, or the sick. Baptists rightly believe that one is justified on the basis of

18. One difference between the likes of Bavinck and Hodge is that they presumed election rather than regeneration. For them, the timing of regeneration was not as important as it seemed to be to Calvin.

faith alone through grace alone. They do not believe that a public profession of faith is needed in order to be justified because this would just be a work that is needed on top of faith. Thus, if faith is the condition for being included within the church and receiving the ordinances therein, then what withholds those who have not professed from being baptized? I would be supportive of the idea of *believers* baptism, but not of the idea of *credo* baptism. To say it another way, the presumption of regeneration is not based upon baptism, but their baptism is based upon this presumption. This is the same rhetoric used by Baptists in their desire to only give the ordinance of baptism to those whom they presume to have been regenerated. In the same way, I would be supportive of *believers* communion, but not the idea of *credo* communion. The Lord's Table is a table for believers who are in proper good standing with the church, not those specially mature believers who are able to evidence their faith in a verbal manner.

This presumption of regeneration found a secure footing in the likes of many Reformed and Puritan divines. An English Puritan rejecting nominalism and experientialism, Thomas Boston advocated that those who, in the judgment of charity, are presumably regenerated should be admitted into baptism and church membership.[19] Calvin makes clear, "the children of believers are baptized *not* in order that they who were previously strangers to the church may then for the first time become children of God, but rather that, because by the blessing of the promise they already belonged to the body of Christ."[20] Similarly, Abraham Kuyper argues, "Calvinists have always taught that baptism should be administered on the presumption that regeneration has preceded . . . [and] stated how God would have us *consider* such infants, and this consideration based on the divine Word made it imperative to look upon their infant children as elect and saved, and to treat them accordingly."[21] Ursinus, the author of the Heidelberg

19. Schenck, *Presbyterian Doctrine*, 54.
20. Calvin, *Institutes* (Battles), 1323.
21. Kuyper, "Calvinism," 388.

Catechism, viewed children of believers as having already entered the process of regeneration before baptism saying,

> Those are not to be excluded from baptism, to whom the benefit of the remission of sins, and of regeneration belongs. But this benefit belongs to the infants of the church; for redemption from sin, by the blood of Christ and the Holy Ghost, the author of faith, is promised to them no less than to the adult. . . . Those unto whom the things signified belong, unto them the sign also belongs . . . baptism ought to be administered to infants also; for they *are* holy; the promise is unto them; the kingdom of heaven *is* theirs; and God, who is certainly not the God of the wicked, declares that he will also be their God. Neither is there any condition in infants which would forbid the use of baptism. Who then can forbid water, or exclude them from baptism, seeing that they *are* partakers with the whole church of the same blessings?[22]

By the testimony of federal headship in the Scriptures and within this judgment of charity upon infants of believers, my Baptist brethren may continue to maintain that the church is still a body of baptized believers—that is, those who are presumed to possess faith. The main questions deal with *who* we are to presume are believers and *when* we ought to presume that they become believers. That is, on what basis do we presume someone to be regenerated? Verbal profession as the standard for infant and adult alike does not follow the logic of Scripture. While appropriate for those who are able to profess, it ought not be required absolutely. Infants of believing parents should be considered regenerated on the basis of God's promise throughout Scripture to be God to believers and their seed (Gen 17:7, Deut 7:9, Ps 103:17, Isa 59:21, Acts 2:39). When Abraham circumcised Isaac it was given to Isaac on the basis of Isaac's presumed faith. "In the very act of circumcision, the profession was made that God was the God of the one circumcised."[23] This is why Rom 4:11 attests that circumcision was

---

22. Ursinus, *Commentary*, 372.
23. Schenck, *Presbyterian Doctrine*, 125.

a *seal* of the faith prior to the circumcision. And this is the precedent taken into the new covenant church as it describes the Abra-
hamic covenant and covenant blessings as finding their essence in
the gospel message (Rom 4:9–12; Gal 3). "Since the promise [and
the seal of the promise—namely, circumcision and baptism] is not
only to parents but to their seed, children are by the command of
God to be regarded and treated as of the number of the elect."[24]
This idea of covenant succession can be aptly compared with the
idea of national citizenship. On the basis of a parent's citizenship,
the child is regarded as a citizen as well. In the same way, on the
basis of a parent's membership with the church, the child is to be
regarded as a member of the church as well. This idea of covenant
succession, though somewhat contrary to western individualism,
is not foreign to the western mind.

While this thinking advocates for a presumption of regeneration *prior to* baptism, the grace bestowed *in* baptism should not
be trivialized. As previously stated, *regeneration* is not univocal in
its usage but has multiple meanings. One such meaning is that we
are brought into a realm through the waters of baptism. In a very
real way, baptism does produce a change of status in the life of
the baptized. Similar to betrothal and marriage, baptism seals a
preexisting relationship by formally bringing the baptized into the
church, the vessel of salvation. The baptized enter a new realm,
as it were, a new creation. Whereas before they are proleptically
united to Christ by faith alone, in baptism they are formally united
to Christ in his death, burial, and resurrection. In this way they
signal to the world that they are united to the firstfruits of the new
creation. This grace given is not merely formal, but enacts a real life
change in the lives of the baptized and the rest of the congregation.
From now on both the newly baptized and the previously baptized
are part of one body, the church, and as such they are to mutually
encourage and challenge each other to stay true to their baptismal
vow. Broadly speaking, Baptists would agree with the sentiment
that baptism changes the roles in which you function within the
church. Prior to it, you were considered an outsider to the church

24. Hodge, "Church Membership of Infants," 375–76.

and given no rights to the table of the Lord and no rights to express change within. But after baptism you are considered an insider and reserve the rights and privileges of anyone else, from the least to the greatest. Far from spiritualizing baptism as a mere picture of God's grace, baptism is a means of grace that implants the baptized into the life of the local congregation, thus formally securing their foothold within the vessel of salvation—the church. Neglecting baptism of the presumably regenerated is akin to those overboard not receiving a life preserver in order to enter the ship. While they are certainly alive by the grace of God, they are at risk of dying if they do not receive the life preserver. Normatively speaking, those who neglect baptism are at a serious risk of not completing their faith because they do not take advantage of the grace given by God *in* the waters of baptism. It ought to be clear by this point that grace is not bestowed *ex opere operato*, but rather the grace of baptism ought to be received by faith (just like the life preserver must be received). The Spirit works in the soul of the baptized to receive the gift with faith in its power and working.

To summarize the matter, our question can be simplified down to the familiar motto in America's judicial system: Should we consider children of believers innocent until proven guilty? Or should we regard them as guilty until proven innocent? The former seems to stand in line with much of the way that God speaks of covenant children, and it is congruent with how Jesus treated little children (Luke 18:16).

Ministerial Challenges for Opponents

Now that we have set forth the concept of presumed regeneration and its natural applications of paedobaptism and paedocommunion, what might be the challenges experienced by opponents of these views? Before I list some of the challenges, these ought not dictate our interpretation of Scripture. We should not advocate for a certain position because it provides less challenges but rather because it is scriptural. So while these challenges should not dictate our views, perhaps they should be treated as warning lights on a car dashboard revealing that some hermeneutical principles are lacking.

Lack of Charity for the Weakest

The first challenge that might plague someone who does not hold to this view of Scripture is how to charitably care for the weakest among us—namely, infants and the mentally incapacitated. If faith is said to only be authentic upon profession, then neither infants nor the mentally incapacitated can possess true faith and thus are lost to eternal damnation upon their death. My Baptist brethren would never make such a statement. Neither would they tell my three-year-old daughter who professes faith in Christ, "No you can't be a Christian, because you are only three years old and cannot make a *credible* profession of faith." How heartless and anti-scriptural would this be? This sentiment has been experienced by far too many, though, within many evangelical churches. My own daughter was denied the bread and cup by an elder of a Presbyterian church because she "looked to young!" Even though she had proudly declared her faith in front of many and had been considered by me as a believer, this elder judged the book by her youthful cover and denied her the opportunity to taste and see that the Lord is good! Does this not go against the basic tenets of Scripture that value faith not according to its maturity but according to its object? Does this not evince the exclusivity of the disciples who prohibited the little children from coming to Christ? Did not Christ make manifestly clear that the kingdom of heaven belongs to such as these? This goes against every bone in the Bible-believing body of my Baptist brothers and sisters who insist on simple child-like faith as a means to justification. If profession is made the standard by which infants are prohibited from being considered possessors of faith, then what ought to be said to the believing parent of a child with autism, Down syndrome, or another mental incapacity that prohibits them from giving a credible profession of faith? Perhaps this view stems from an incorrect and narrow interpretation on what it means to "call upon the name of the Lord." If we truly believe that salvation is by grace through faith, then what is the scriptural basis that prohibits the infant or mentally incapacitated child of believing parents from being considered as possessing the seeds of regenerative faith?

Furthermore, making subjective judgment calls on the faith of these weakest among us may in fact lead to an insecurity later in their life that causes them to seek after other security apart from the church and the gospel in which they were told as children they had no part. If they are told that they cannot lay claim to Christ until they have some existential experience of true conversion, then what will hold them steadfast during a season of spiritual drought? Trouwborst's statement about the current state of the church is all too familiar for many grieving parents and church members who have seen their child walk away from the faith: "To view, treat, and teach our children as aliens to the church has become a self-fulfilling prophecy."[25] The Scriptures are clear, God wants Christians to *regard* their children as Christians.

On a similar note, why do many paedobaptists feel content providing the children of believers with the ordinance of initiation, but not the ordinance of perseverance? Would they ever give the Supper to the mentally incapacitated who has been baptized? If not, how heartless this would be! They deserve a seat at the table even though they are not physically able to profess their faith.

Susceptibility to Experientialism

The next challenge for those who do not hold to this view is the susceptibility to experientialism. The tendency to assure someone's salvation by calling them to harken back to the hazy memory of the sinner's prayer they said in the pews during their earliest days can be quite offsetting. What if they do not remember their experience? What assurance do they have for their faith if it was prior to their "mature doctrinal understanding" that they have in the present?

---

25. Trouwborst, "Covenant to Chaos," 102.

My Baptist pastor was very helpful to me as I considered my younger days, which I constituted to be an inadequate representation of authentic faith. He told me not to underestimate the seedlike faith that was present during my younger days, and warned me to withhold setting up an experiential standard, which twenty years from now might also look like an inadequate representation of authentic faith. On top of this, there runs the risk of elevating experience to the point where people chase after experience artificially by the means of any number of charismatic routes. In this, the church is then a place for those spiritually elite who *actually* experience the joy of their salvation, rather than those who are in a long season of wilderness times with the Lord. The opponent of a covenantal view of Scripture will inevitably promote "an unhealthy overemphasis on the subjective element of the covenant, and with a standard often beyond what the Bible requires."[26] The requirement for profession of faith is even found to be disregarded by many baptistic churches who require a vivid conversion experience from a teenager rather than a simple profession that "Jesus is Lord" from the lips of a three-year-old. Not only this, but the proponent of the credo position unknowingly sets up a system similar to the Roman Catholic understanding of confirmation, where the priest decides who is mature enough in the faith to be considered a full member of the church. My Baptist brethren ought to recoil at this perverse, stale, and subjective standard laid upon those within the Roman Catholic church. As Atwater notes,

> Whether one remembers the time and manner of the beginning and progressive development of these states of mind and heart, or whether these have ingrained themselves so imperceptibly into the warp and woof of his inner being that he can mark no distinct epoch or hinge-point in his career, as the crisis of the new birth, it is enough that he can say, "I am a child of God."[27]

Some might thoughtfully read this and ask about the age of discernment and why there is a different treatment of the adult

26. Trouwborst, "Covenant to Chaos," 102.
27. Atwater, "Children of the Church," 92.

convert to the faith. Why would a profession of faith be appropriate from those who are able to profess and not from the infants or mentally incapacitated children of believers? If the distinction between infants of believers and adult pagan converts has not already been made clear, perhaps then it would be clear from Paul's declaration in 2 Thess 3:10. If infants and adults are to be treated equally in the church, then infants, who do not work for their living, ought not to eat! Obviously we do not require infants to work in order to eat because they are unable.

A person's involvement in baptism and the Lord's Supper ought not be predicated upon a profession of faith or some vivid experience. Rather, to the extent that we are able to confess, we should confess. To the extent that we are able to testify to experience, we should testify. But we should not prohibit those who cannot profess their faith or testify to some dramatic conversion experience. Even though we do not remember when our parents became our parents, it does not make them any less our parents. In the same way, even if we are not to remember when God became our Father, it does not mean that we are any less his child.

Deficiency in Pastoral Care

Another challenge that will be experienced by those who oppose this view is in the arena of pastoral care. There are many situations of suffering that can arise in the church that would provide a dangerous challenge not only to the pastor but to any Christian layman who denies this covenantal view.

How do you counsel the believing parents who have lost an infant to miscarriage or who have a mentally incapable child who has passed away? Would God send these covenant children to hell? Salvation is by grace alone through faith alone, not through youth alone. Therefore, many within the Baptist camp would fall upon the mercy of God to save these children, but on what basis do they do this except on the presumed regeneration that instills faith—the same thing for which I argue?

Another situation that is difficult to treat pastorally without this view is that of apostasy. How do you care for your flock in the midst of a trusted elder who professed his faith and served faithfully for decades only to give up on his faith? How do you treat passages in the Scripture that warn about apostasy without doing hermeneutical violence to them? How can Heb 10:29–31 tell us that there were some who were sanctified who proceeded to trample upon the Son of God? How can Heb 6:4–6 tell us that there are some who have tasted the heavenly gift and shared in the Holy Spirit only to have fallen away? Why would the apostle Paul warn that God will not spare the proud church members in Rom 11:13–21? As it pertains to the issue of apostasy, the covenantal view of Scripture provides a basis for someone experiencing the covenantal union without experiencing the vital union.[28] To be a part of the church is really to experience the corporate salvation and the benefits of the Spirit. And yet to fall away from this experience of salvation is something seen in churches in every age, thus evidencing that those individuals were not specially elect. The opponents of this covenantal view will have to lean on 1 John 2:19 to substantiate their view that they were never of the flock even though experience and a greater amount of scriptural proof would tell us differently.[29]

Platonistic Dualism

There is a tendency for those who do not subscribe to this view to see a dichotomy between the spiritual and material realms. Seeing the church as the distinctively spiritual purpose of God they fail to see the Platonistic dualism at the root of their theology. In this thinking the old covenant was the physical covenant pertaining to

28. For more on the different types of faith and their connection to apostasy see Lusk's *Paedofaith: A Primer on the Mystery of Infant Salvation and a Handbook for Covenant Parents.*

29. Exegetically and grammatically, it is possible that 1 John 2:19 says "they ceased to be part of us," rather than "they never were part of us." ἦσαν could be interpreted as a negation of the iterative imperfect.

the flesh and the new covenant is the spiritual covenant for a pecu-
liarly spiritual people. Distinct from this, "covenant theology does
not see redemption as related to a more 'spiritual' realm . . . [but]
from the perspective of creation. No dichotomy exists ultimately
between redemption in the spiritual realm and redemption in the
physical realm."[30] The opponents of this covenantal view often
express that God has two eternal purposes, one for the people of
God under the old covenant, and one for the people of God under
the new covenant. Michael Horton makes a compelling case by
connecting Amos 9:11–12 to the apostle James's interpretation of
its fulfillment during the Jerusalem Council in Acts 15:14–18.[31]
Seeing that James saw the fulfillment of Israel's rebuilding through
the lens of the Great Commission to the gentiles, it leaves little
room to divide the rebuilding of Israel from the building of Christ's
kingdom, the church. To do so is to unintentionally take the focus
off of salvation through Jesus Christ. "There are not two centers to
Scripture, Israel and Jesus Christ, but one."[32] And seeing that no
Baptist wants to take the focus off of Christ, this dualistic perspective does not prove to be sufficient. All the covenants of God, both
the old and the new, find their consummation in the person and
works of Jesus Christ. And moreover, all physical creation is being
redeemed and renewed.

Additionally, there is even a dualistic tendency among
many modern Presbyterians that view children baptized into the
church, not as presumably regenerated in a vital way, but rather
as those who are a part of an external ecclesial institution from
which the vitally regenerated are taken. Schenck summarizes the
downward trajectory of thought among Presbyterian circles as to
the sealing significance of baptism:

> The visible church was not a group of those who were
> presumably true children of God, but a field out of
> which the true children of God were called, an institu-
> tion in which they were trained. . . . [Baptized children]

30. Robertson, *Christ of the Covenants*, 213.

31. Horton, *Pilgrim*, 438.

32. Horton, *Pilgrim*, 439.

were introduced into an "ecclesiastical covenant," into the visible church, but *not* on the basis that they were presumptively God's children. . . . In the case of an infant, it was believed to be only a sign of the spiritual blessings which he would receive when growing older, provided he believed. In the case of an adult entering the church on a profession of faith in Christ, baptism was held to signify that which presumably was true in his case, his spiritual renewal, ingrafting in Christ, etc.[33]

Whether paedobaptist or credobaptist, we need to protect ourselves from the tendency to separate the material from the spiritual. We are body *and* soul, and the great plan of salvation is to redeem both through the person and work of Jesus Christ.

Ministerial Benefits for Advocates

There are also benefits for advocates of the position. Again we ought not be so teleological in our thinking that the ends justify the means, but the benefits can serve as an assurance that the car of our theology is running smoothly because we are running on the correct doctrinal fuel.

Scripturally Accurate Pastoral Exhortations

This covenantal perspective is able to sustain a pastoral handling of the Scriptures. It accurately balances assurance and warning. Assurance is for the specially elect who cannot be taken out of the hand of Christ. For those whose faith is predestined to endure, there is an unshakable certainty at their disposal. However, the Scriptures often do not make mention of the predestined endurance of the few, but rather admonish endurance among the many. Because the elect remnant is unknown in the absolute sense, the apostles warn the covenant people of God about the risk of falling away and becoming covenant breakers. While these warnings are prominent in the

33. Schenck, *Presbyterian Doctrine*, 86–87.

Scriptures, the emphasis of God's word is on the positive promises to his covenant people. Thus, the pastor is able to treat all within the covenant community as if they are the elect of God.

> The people of God need to hear themselves spoken of and to as God's elect, as his children, as those bought with the price of Christ's blood, as those renewed and indwelt by the Spirit. Otherwise, the "doctrines of grace" remain an abstraction, removed from our experience, and the truths of God's sovereignty in salvation cannot comfort us. The Reformed church usually uses very direct language in talking about sin ("You're a sinner! You're guilty before God!"). But when we turn to talk about the gospel, we suddenly become impersonal and abstract ("Christ died for the elect, whoever they are. . . . Those the Father chose are regenerated by the Spirit"). This impersonal language is bound to feed doubt and despair among God's children and is the result of failing to take covenant theology seriously.[34]

At the same time this covenantal view necessitates that we take the warnings seriously. Even the apostle Paul lived with a proper balance of assurance and healthy fear. "Our attitude should be like that of Paul, who knew he belonged to the Lord (e.g., 2 Tim. 1, 4:6ff), and yet lived in healthy fear of the danger of falling away (1 Cor. 9:24–27)."[35] The Bible does not give us an age after which the believer must never worry about apostatizing from the faith because he can rely on his faith that was deemed as credible upon his mature profession. Salvation is not merely seen in a "Once saved always saved" light, but rather salvation is viewed eschatologically in which vital justification is the basis and motivation for the perseverance that results in salvation. This covenantal perspective is able to sustain a scripturally accurate pastoral balance of assurance and warning.

34. Lusk, "Covenant and Election."
35. Lusk, "Covenant and Election."

Strong Nuclear Family

This view also strengthens the nuclear family in an age that rejects it. Instead of an individualistic approach in which a person must relate to God outside of the influence of family relationship, societal location, and covenantal structures, the covenantal structure sees the importance of the family, and in particular the father, in a way that is opposed to the "crudely modern" individualistic approach.[36] Of course Satan wants to attack the family and its consequential place in the eternal life of its children. Satan always desires to destroy the most influential instruments in God's kingdom, so it makes sense that he would desire to individualize children from their parents in order that he might destroy the nuclear family. In strong opposition to Satan's plan, we must recognize the significance that parents have in the piety of their children. The display of your faith before your children matters. The decisions you make for how to educate and nurture your children matter. Catechizing your children regularly matters. Disciplining your children for disobedience matters. Comforting your children during times of hardship and suffering matters. The Lord has given much responsibility to parents in nurturing their children and molding them into people who fear the Lord. While the ultimate power to mold the child into the image of Jesus Christ relies upon the Holy Spirit, the parents have a great responsibility in being the vessel for such a work. Conversely, your upbringing in a church-going family matters and ought not be denigrated as a sterile meaningless ritual. Children who grow up in a family that faithfully attends church are in the minority, and those children ought to be thankful that God blessed them with such a gift rather than turning to experientialism and spurning the faith of their parents.

The covenantal view approaches the nuclear family in such a way that there is no small connection between the faith of the parents and the faith of the children. And while it is not the sole instrument that God uses for his divine purpose, it is of

36. Gibson, "Fathers of Faith," 21.

vast importance. "Christian nurture [is], then, the appointed, the natural, the normal, and ordinary means by which the children of believers [are] made truly the children of God."[37] Baptists make much effort to provide the appropriate structures for their children to succeed and grow into mature Christians. This covenantal view simply strengthens the opinion that, *normatively speaking*, Christian parents are congruent with or lead to Christian children.

Gospel Relevance

As opposed to a reliance upon the past or some future experience of grace, the covenantal view stresses the need to apprehend God's promises *today*. Some who argue that the covenantal view diminishes the need to preach the gospel to the covenant children wholly misrepresent the Reformed cause. The gospel is for each and every Christian for each and every day. May I never wake up and claim that I do not need the gospel as much as the unconverted pagan. Perhaps this is the importance of defining regeneration as a lifelong process that is synonymous with the presence of faith rather than as a single event at a point in time. Rather than making people new, regeneration *re*news people. Every day we ought to revisit the cleansing fountain of the gospel in order to drink deeply from it and to sustain us during our brief sojourn in this world of sin. Faith in the gospel is like breathing, without it we die. Thus, regeneration is the process by which we constantly express faith in the gospel throughout our entire lives.

Covenant children who are presumed to possess faith ought to be taught each day to consider and lay hold of the gospel. Contrary to an experientialist approach that has the tendency to rely on previous or future graces, the covenantal view gives promises for the day similar to the manna given to the Israelites in the wilderness. Thus, the gospel not only provides the basis for justification but also for sanctification! My Baptist brethren continually focus on the fundamentals of the faith in their worship

37. Schenck, *Presbyterian Doctrine*, 145.

services in a way that glorifies God by attracting the nonbeliever and exhorting the believer in a contemporary way. So this type of thinking is not foreign to them as they consider the gospel as the grounds for justification and sanctification.

Importance of the Church

Finally, this covenantal view stresses the necessity of the church. In a real way the church is the vessel of salvation, and *normatively*, those outside of her do not have a claim upon salvation. Thus, persistent and eager involvement in the church is needed to persevere in the faith. There is an unassailable connection between church participation and salvation. Those who are not in the visible covenant people of God are in danger of eternal damnation. Although God can save outside the means of the church in drastic situations, his *normative* approach is to save through the church. As the Westminster Confession of Faith says, "The visible church, which is also catholic or universal under the gospel (not confined to one nation, as before under the law), consists of all those throughout the world that profess the true religion; and of their children: and is the kingdom of the Lord Jesus Christ, the house and family of God, out of which there is no ordinary possibility of salvation."[38] In this way, the ordinances and the preached word of God, which are only sanctioned in the church, take a special place as the primary means through which people are ultimately saved. Faithful participation in the communion of the saints is God's primary means of saving the elect. And this progressive participation ought to start from the first breath of the infant of believers.

Furthermore, in order to protect from the nominalism that might threaten this type of ordinance- and word-centered church, discipline then becomes a much more meaningful means of helping someone mature in their faith. Rather than seeing church discipline as a negative, we ought to see it as the Scriptures testify about it—namely, that it is the loving hand of

---

38. Westminster Assembly, *Westminster Confession of Faith*, 120.

the heavenly Father bringing us back to himself (Heb 12:5–11). If someone is expressing nominalism in their faith, if they are spurning the gathering together on a normal basis, if they are living a licentious lifestyle, then it is the church's duty to bring discipline against this member as a way to protect that individual and to protect the church against nominalism.

In other words, paedo-administration of the ordinances protects from experientialism while formal church discipline protects from nominalism. Perhaps the minimization of the church is why we see much less formal discipline exercised within her walls. Very few denominations value church involvement and membership as highly as my Baptist brethren, so this covenantal view only elevates this thinking by showing that church membership and involvement is congruent with eternal individual election. Thus, discipline ought to be faithfully and consistently carried out against the church's members in a case-appropriate way. In this way, a child of faith would not be held to the same standard of belief and practice as the mature believer who knows better. This is the Biblical doctrine of spiritual nurture, and is fitting to the general scheme of life. However, denominationalism perpetuates the evangelical church culture that lacks discipline. If a member is disciplined and excommunicated from one denomination in town, he or she can then just take a few steps to a church in a different denomination and find a place within the congregation. This is an obvious chink in the armor of evangelical churches. If these churches were united across denominational lines discipline would be enacted in a way in which those being disciplined could not side step. In this way the church is able to unite in the reformation of the disciplinee's soul.

Conservative Evangelical Church Union

HAVING LAID OUT THE biblical, historical, and theological warrants for my desire to see a conservative evangelical reunion, is it possible to rectify the culture of denominationalism within the evangelical church? Can the curse of Jeroboam and Novatian be reversed? Many have tried and failed, and while I am not naive to believe that this proposal will solve the issue, perhaps it can help by generating ecumenical thinking. Some may call this an idealist notion incapable of any enduring success. The following evangelical ecumenical ecclesiology is ideal, but this does not mean it is impossible. The very fact that most readers would call it an "idealist" approach shows that it is a core desire of many evangelical Christians and therefore "has the legs" to be accomplished.

Reasonable Christians are tired of squabbling with each other over non-fundamental issues and would rather band together to produce a Biblically sound, conscience-liberating ecclesiology that shows the world the nature of the love spoken by our Lord in the seventeenth chapter of the Gospel of John. Conservative evangelical churches grounded in the gospel of grace ought to form a unified front against her enemy forces instead of quarreling with each other over reasonable assessments about the ordinances of the church. We should take a page out of Irenaeus's book, who outlined gracious bounds of orthodoxy in the midst of the gnostic heresies so long ago.[1]

The future of an evangelical reunion is possible so long as we provide liberty within the realm of orthodoxy. This does not mean everyone must agree in their interpretation or conclusion, but rather that charity ought to be practiced toward those of differing convictions within the realm of orthodoxy. As Shields so rightly notes,

> Church unity should be distinguished still further from Church uniformity. . . . [Church uniformity] would reduce all Christian bodies to one type of doctrine, polity, and worship. . . . Absolute uniformity is not possible either in the world of nature or of grace. . . . All experience shows that a rigid uniformity in doctrine and ritual could only breed dissent and schism.[2]

The following proposal provides conservative evangelicals an example for how to maintain a balance between non-fundamental

1. "The Church, though dispersed throughout the whole world, even to the ends of the earth, has received from the apostles and their disciples this faith: [She believes] in one God, the Father Almighty, Maker of heaven, and earth, and the sea, and all things that are in them; and in one Christ Jesus, the Son of God, who became incarnate for our salvation; and in the Holy Spirit, who proclaimed through the prophets the dispensations of God, and the advents, and the birth from a virgin, and the passion, and the resurrection from the dead, and the ascension into heaven in the flesh of the beloved Christ Jesus, our Lord, and His [future] manifestation from heaven in the glory of the Father 'to gather all things in one,' and to raise up anew all flesh of the whole human race, in order that to Christ Jesus, our Lord, and God, and Saviour, and King, according to the will of the invisible Father, 'every knee should bow, of things in heaven, and things in earth, and things under the earth, and that every tongue should confess' to Him, and that He should execute just judgment towards all; that He may send spiritual wickednesses, and the angels who transgressed and became apostates, together with the ungodly, and unrighteous, and wicked, and profane among men, into everlasting fire; but may, in the exercise of His grace, confer immortality on the righteous, and holy, and those who have kept His commandments, and have persevered in His love, some from the beginning [of their Christian course], and others from [the date of] their repentance, and may surround them with everlasting glory." Irenaeus, *Against Heresies*, 330–31; brackets original.

2. Shields, *Historic Episcopate*, 6–7.

diversity and fundamental uniformity. It is my conviction that a moderated episcopal approach to governance is the most promising option for such a conservative evangelical movement.[3]

Ideal Scenario

In each city or region church leaders should work with one another under the bond of unity in order to spread the gospel message and grow the kingdom of Christ, while also holding out the freedom to follow one's own conscience on non-fundamental issues. Rather than having separate churches in which the doctrine of either the Presbyterian, Baptist, Lutheran, or Methodist tradition is echoed throughout its chambers, there ought to be elders at each church with varying persuasions on the proper administration of the ordinances. In one locale, a church family would be pastored by congregationally elected Baptist and Presbyterian ministers. Another church within the same geographic area would be pastored by congregationally elected Lutheran and Methodist ministers.[4] Along with these teaching elders (pastors) there would be other ruling elders that are similarly elected by the congregation. In proportion to their size, each congregation would be given a certain number of votes by which their elected elders would choose a regional presiding chairman who would be the emblem of unity between the various regional congregations. This chairman would be considered alongside the other elders in this region as "first among equals." That is, his jurisdiction would primarily be considered as an organizational administration that would entail ordaining the elected elders for each congregation and enforcing the agreed upon doctrine

3. Though the preference is given to the episcopal form of governance, the following proposal advocates for a mixture of all three normative forms of governance: episcopal, presbyterian, and congregational.

4. For those concerned about doctrinal purity, consider the following from C. W. Shields: "Exact theological agreement has never existed; not even in the Apostolic church, which allowed doctrinal differences without the unchristian results of schism and sectarianism. . . . Better that two schools of theology should fairly contend in the same church than rush apart into two hostile sects." Shields, *Historic Episcopate*, 35.

of regional councils. The agreed upon doctrines by which he would be bound in his duties to enforce would be decided at a regional council. These councils would arise when there is disagreement as to which situations deserve liberty at the congregational level and which situations would warrant agreement across all congregations.[5] These councils would establish unifying doctrinal standards that limit their scope to the basic evangelical tenants upon which all can agree—some examples of these are the Nicene Creed, Apostles' Creed, the Definition of Chalcedon, the Chicago Statement on Biblical Inerrancy, and the Nashville Statement on Biblical Manhood and Womanhood. In order to sanction the doctrines, these councils would need two-thirds support from a representation of the laity, elders, and chairmen alike. Toon advocates for this moderated type of episcopal government when he says, "It is preferable to speak of synodical government rather than episcopal government. A synod [council] consists of a house of bishops [chairmen], a house of clergy [elders], and a house of laity [congregation]. Major decisions have to be supported by all of these houses. In contrast, lower clergy and laity do not have the same full participation in church government in either the Orthodox or the Roman Catholic churches where a synod consists only of bishops."[6]

5. A similar process is currently done through a primarily presbyterian form of government by the Communion of Reformed Evangelical Churches. Churches within this federation are free to subscribe to paedo or credo usage of the ordinances while maintaining union with one another as to the fundamentals subscribed in the Nicene Creed, the Apostles' Creed, and the Definition of Chalcedon. See Communion, *Governing Documents*.

6. Cowan, *4 Views*, 23.

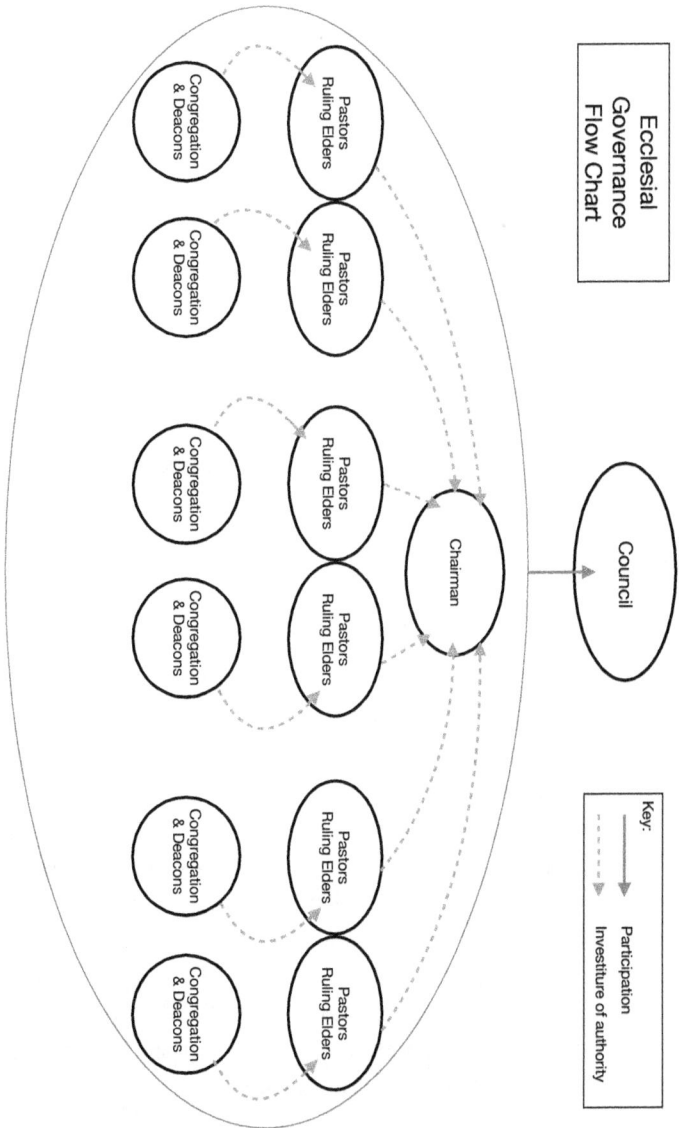

Ecclesial Governance Flow Chart

Congregation & Deacons

Pastors Ruling Elders

Chairman

Council

Key:

Participation

Investiture of authority

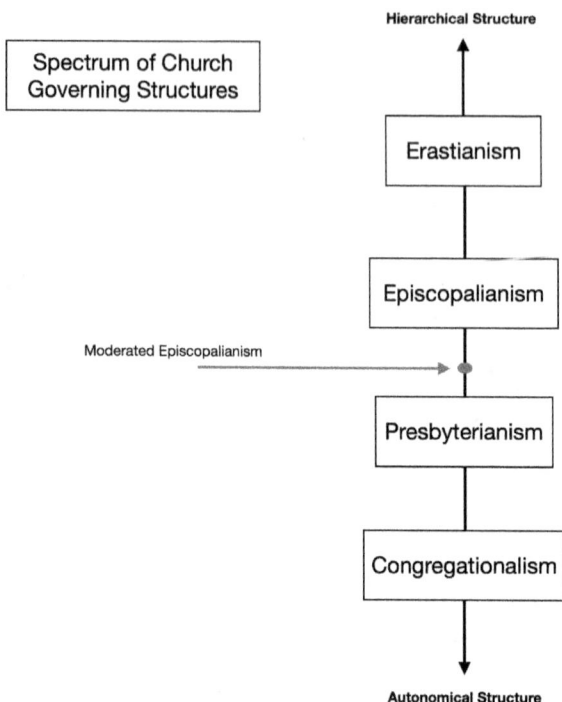

"What worldly men have done in their political relations, cannot Christian men do in their religious relations?"[7] This proposed system of governance reflects our national governance in that it has a system of checks and balances that procure both progressivism and conservatism. The laity would vote into office their elders (Congress). These elders would then be given proportionate votes (electoral college) by which they would honor the desires of their constituents in electing a chairman (President).[8] And this chairman would be limited in his enforcement by the councils (Supreme Court). With a proper system of checks and balances, the superiors are given authority by their parishioners by which the church would benefit from a unified front in which the

7. Shields, *Historic Episcopate*, 14.

8. Each congregation would be given a minimum number of votes to ensure that they are not overlooked because of their size.

fundamentals are celebrated while the whole counsel of God is left up to the conscience of the ministers within each church. Obviously this would require a two way street of humility. It would require submissive investiture from congregants to their elders and chairman, and it would require humble leadership that does not abuse its powers. Accordingly, it would require a procedure for expulsion of leaders who betray the requirements of their office. If the core of the Christian faith is retained I see nothing that should sanction the divisiveness seen within Bible-heralding conservative evangelical churches today. Rather, differing expressions of the same fundamental faith ought to be sanctioned within all churches under the banner of brotherly affection. Rather than seeing the dividing line between doctrinal minutiae, these churches would see a dividing line between belief and unbelief. John Frame eloquently summarizes this view:

> In view of our Lord's Great Commission, our concern should be, not merely with that portion of the community which belongs to our tradition, but with the community at large, Christian and non-Christian. With that outlook, we can see that there really need be no competition at all. For no denomination can possibly do the whole job. When we see the dimensions of the evangelistic task before us, we will be thankful that there are denominations besides our own to help out.[9]

The following analysis will provide the Biblical, historical, and theological precedents that inform this proposed church polity in hopes that it will be considered a reasonable practice to implement within the reader's own context.

Biblical Precedents

Aside from the numerous passages that discuss the principle of Christian unity and love that motivates *why* we should pursue ecumenical ecclesiology (e.g., John 17 and Eph 4), there are apostolic

9. Frame, *Evangelical Reunion*, 38.

doctrines that note *how* to practically navigate this complicated mandate. It would be an obvious case of presentism to assume that the church today experiences the threat of disunity more than the apostolic church. Many passages testify to the seeds of discord in various churches that were dealt with in an orderly manner via apostolic ecclesiological dictates. However, the specifics of church polity are not invariably clear. This lack of clarity has led to a debate among three reputable evangelical theories of church polity: congregational, presbyterian, and episcopal.

The central questions that delineate each of these forms are *who rules the church* and *how are leaders appointed.*[10] That is, how do the Scriptures speak about the organism of the church in terms of practical leadership and organization? It is worth noting that each of these forms agree on at least two offices within church government—namely, the office of πρεσβύτερος and διάκονος. The questions up for debate are: (1) Are the offices in the church limited to these? (2) Who has the primal authority in times of dissension? And (3) who has the responsibility to appoint authority?

Some of the most noteworthy passages that illuminate some answers for this study are found in Acts 20:17–28; Titus 1:5–9; 1 Tim 3:1—5:17; Phil 1:1; and 1 Pet 5:1–2. These passages provide some descriptive information on church polity in the nascent church, but do not prescribe specifics. And therein we find the root of dissension. While it is unlikely that these passages will absolutely clarify the prescriptive form of the church, they will at least partially inform how we ought to think about the offices of ἐπίσκοπος, πρεσβύτερος and διάκονος. In so doing, it will provide a foundation for ecumenism by unifying on perspicuous matters and charitably conceding on unclear matters.

It is likely that the formal offices in the church as elucidated in the Scripture were limited to two—the deacon and the presbyter. Calvin makes an extensive remark on the opening verse of Paul to the Philippian church. In it he clarifies what he believes

---

10. While Christ is certainly the head of the church, this concept of "ruling" considers how his rule is expressed on earth through the church and her elected leaders.

to be a synonymous usage between overseer and elder. He quotes Jerome as the premier church father who showed that the hierarchy between bishop and elder was introduced later on and "rests on no Scripture authority."[11] Thereafter he commends the necessity of establishing an elder who presides over other elders, but in so doing he also somewhat alludes to a congregational approach to church polity when he says that this presidency should be restricted to "particular bodies, not of whole provinces, much less of the whole world."[12]

In his estimation of Acts 20:28, Vincent clarifies that ἐπισκόπους describes "the official function of the elders, but not in the later ecclesiastical sense of bishops, as implying an order distinct from elders. The two terms are synonymous. The elders, by virtue of their office, were overseers."[13] He also notes the cultural precedents of the day when he says, "Those who are called elder in speaking of Jewish communities are called bishops in speaking of gentile communities. Hence the latter term prevails in Paul's epistles."[14]

Similar to Vincent, in his exposition of Acts 20:28 Bruce sees no distinction between the titles of presbyter and bishop "such as we find from the second century onwards."[15] However he does note the "appointment" of such elders by the apostles during the process of planting new churches, making it very clear that this appointment was done in the context of missionary activity and not necessarily to be seen as a prescription for founded churches.[16]

In his analysis on the form of the church in his seminal work on inaugurated eschatology, Ladd suggests that since the participle προϊστάμενοι is used in 1 Timothy, Romans, and 1 Thessalonians in reference to bishops, deacons, and elders, "there is good reason to conclude that προϊστάμενοι designates the office of elder-bishop

11. Calvin, *Commentary*, 23.

12. Calvin, *Commentary*, 23.

13. Vincent, *Word Studies*, 1:561.

14. Vincent, *Word Studies*, 1:523.

15. Bruce, *Acts*, 415.

16. Bruce, *Acts*, 296.

and deacon."[17] He extrapolates that "in the apostolic fathers, especially in Ignatius, the bishop emerges as distinct and superior to the elders, giving rise to the office of monarchical bishop."[18] He does concede that one ought not be dogmatic about the apostolic understanding of church polity by saying, "It is not clear whether there was a single elder-bishop over each local congregation or a college of elders as in the Jewish synagogue (e.g., Luke 22:66)."[19] In his conclusion he argues that there was no normative pattern of church government in the apostolic age and that church polity dwells within the sphere of adiaphora. "It is important to understand that unity does not mean organizational uniformity."[20]

In their note to Titus 1:7 the editors of the NET Bible argue that ἐπίσκοπος is another term for the same official position of leadership as πρεσβύτερος. They validate this claim by citing how the two terms are used interchangeably in Acts 20:17 and 28, as well as the parallels seen between the qualifications listed for these overseers in Titus 1 and those listed for the elders in 1 Tim 3.[21]

Forbes uses his expertise in syntactical and linguistic work to note that the elder possesses the role of oversight, although he strays away from classifying this usage of the term πρεσβύτερος as an example of Peter establishing a prescriptive hierarchical position within the church. Rather he says that "the lack of the definite article points to the term being used in a rather loose way and not as it would be in later Christian literature as part of a developed hierarchical leadership."[22] While not negating the idea of formally expressed offices within the historic church he does not see the need to recognize this as an instance of such.

Even the episcopal-oriented Anglican priest J. B. Lightfoot contends for the scant evidence within the Scriptures for the threefold office. He provides what has been one of the most

17. Ladd, *Theology*, 577.
18. Ladd, *Theology*, 578.
19. Ladd, *Theology*, 579.
20. Ladd, *Theology*, 579.
21. Grassmick et al., NET Bible, 2281.
22. Forbes, *1 Peter*, 166.

influential treatises on this discussion in his commentary to the book of Philippians. In it he substantiates the office of presbyter by aligning it with the Jewish precedent of elder before it. "With the synagogue itself [the church] would naturally, if not necessarily, adopt the normal government of a synagogue, and a body of elders or presbyters would be chosen to direct the religious worship and partly also to watch over the temporal well-being of the society."[23] He then advocates, similar to Vincent, that on the basis of Phil 1:1 the role of bishop was a term used synonymously for presbyter specifically in the gentile churches.[24] By referencing Phil 1:1, Acts 20:17–28, 1 Timothy compared with 1 Peter, and Titus 1:7, he shows that Asia Minor, Crete, and Philippi preferred the term ἐπίσκοπος rather than πρεσβύτερος. He contends *bishop* is particularly a Hellenistic word.[25] He concludes "the two lower orders of the threefold ministry were firmly and widely established; but traces of the third and highest order, the episcopate properly so called, are few and indistinct."[26] On the origin of the episcopate he states that it "was formed not out of the apostolic order by localization but out of the presbytery by elevation."[27] He says that the development of the episcopate was a necessary practical office due to the apostles' limited opportunity to travel and stay with the vast extent of the churches throughout the known world. "It is plainly competent for the Church at any given time to entrust a particular office with larger powers, as the emergency may require."[28]

Therefore the question centers on the transition between the canon of Scripture and the legitimacy of the episcopal form of church governance expressed in the extant writings of the apostolic fathers. Lightfoot appears to be the most adept at analyzing the Scriptures and apostolic fathers in a fair and balanced manner. His treatise was most agreeable in that it argued for the scant

---

23. Lightfoot, "Christian Ministry," 192.
24. Lightfoot, "Christian Ministry," 193.
25. Lightfoot, "Christian Ministry," 194.
26. Lightfoot, "Christian Ministry," 195.
27. Lightfoot, "Christian Ministry," 196.
28. Lightfoot, "Christian Ministry," 244.

evidence for the episcopacy in the Scripture while still holding onto the validity of the episcopate for doctrinal purity throughout an exponentially growing Christendom. Thus it seems while the episcopacy is not within the realm of *esse* as it pertains to church offices, perhaps it is best described as *bene esse* in the early church. However, the level of authority given to this episcopate is so nuanced that a rash appropriation of monarchical authority to the bishops rather than simple precedence among equals will almost certainly devolve into prelacy and sacerdotalism.

Even though there is limited precedent for an episcopal form of governance in the Scripture, it seems proper to advocate for a system like this in times of emergency and division. Thus in our information-heavy internationally diverse world, it may be appropriate to establish a nuanced form of episcopacy for the health and well being of conservative evangelical Christendom.

Historical Precedents

While there is limited evidence for a threefold office in the Scriptures, it is entirely clear that the apostolic fathers had established a formal threefold office by the second century. This historical precedent will provide a reputable footing for a moderated form of episcopacy in evangelical circles. However, on the basis of church history, rather than arguing for the episcopacy as part of the *esse* (essence) of the church, an episcopal form of governance ought to be considered the *bene esse* (well being) of the church. The following analysis of the history of the episcopacy will validate this argument by tracing its development and processes.

The Didache (80–120) was one of the earliest documents during the patristic age, and it only refers to the twofold office of the church when it says, "Therefore appoint for yourselves bishops and deacons worthy of the Lord."[29] The Didache seems to limit itself to the scripturally warranted positions in the church.

---

29. Holmes, *Apostolic Fathers*, 170.

However, around the same time period Clement (70–100) advocated for the episcopacy while shedding some light on the process of appointment:

> Our apostles also knew, through our Lord Jesus Christ, that there would be strife on account of the office of the episcopate. For this reason, therefore, in as much as they had obtained a perfect foreknowledge of this, they appointed those [ministers] already mentioned, and afterwards gave instructions, that when these should fall asleep, other approved men should succeed them in their ministry. We are of opinion, therefore, that those appointed by them, or afterwards by other eminent men, with the consent of the whole Church, and who have blamelessly served the flock of Christ in a humble, peaceable, and disinterested spirit, and have for a long time possessed the good opinion of all, cannot be justly dismissed from the ministry.[30]

What is of note here is the association of the bishop with the apostolic ministry and the means of appointing a new bishop. First we see that the succeeding men were "approved" and then we see that this approval took place "with consent of the whole Church." This shows that the broader congregation was very much a part of the appointment process for the bishop and that the later top down approach was not deemed the best practice.

Ignatius (85–115) is one of the earliest and most eager supporters of the threefold office of the church. An outspoken advocate for the primacy of the bishop, he saw the bishop as the center for Christian unity. "For as many as are of God and of Jesus Christ are also with the bishop."[31] He went so far as to say that any church without a bishop forfeits her position as a true church. In another letter he makes clear his stance in the following: "See that ye all follow the bishop, even as Jesus Christ does the Father, and the presbytery as ye would the apostles; and reverence the deacons, as

---

30. Clement, *First Epistle*, 17; brackets original.
31. Ignatius, *Epistle to the Philadelphians*, 80.

being the institution of God. Let no man do anything connected with the Church without the bishop."[32]

Irenaeus (150–200) is another patristic bishop whose view on the episcopacy is somewhat unclear. In discussing the arrogance of the gnostics he limits his appeal to two offices within the church: "But when again we appeal against them to that tradition which is derived from the Apostles, which is preserved in the churches by successions of presbyters, they place themselves in opposition to it, saying that they, being wiser not only than the presbyters but even than the Apostles, have discovered the genuine truth."[33] Irenaeus seems to again equate the position of presbyter and bishop by using them interchangeably when referring to their succession against the gnostics:

> When we refer them to that tradition which originates from the apostles, [and] which is preserved by means of the succession of presbyters in the Churches, they object to tradition, saying, "It is within the power of all, therefore, in every Church, who may wish to see the truth, to contemplate clearly the tradition of the apostles manifested throughout the whole world; and we are in a position to reckon up those who were by the apostles instituted bishops in the Churches, and [to demonstrate] the succession of these men to our own times.[34]

He attaches the perseverance of the apostolic doctrine to the episcopate when he says that the faith "comes down to our time by means of the successions of the bishops."[35] Whether or not he equated the two will be left up to the reader as it seems to me that one could argue either perspective reasonably.

Cyprian (245–260) was a staunch advocate for the episcopal nature of the church. He ultimately believed that the church was to be identified with the bishop. This makes more sense when considering the Novatian schism that caused him to advocate for

32. Ignatius, *Epistle to the Smyrnaeans*, 89.
33. Irenaeus, *Against Heresies*, 415.
34. Irenaeus, *Against Heresies*, 415.
35. Irenaeus, *Against Heresies*, 415.

the true church in the midst of the divide. It is worth noting that he writes about the normative approach to establishing elders and bishops within the church saying that "the priest should be chosen in the presence of the people under the eyes of all, and should be approved worthy and suitable by public judgment and testimony."[36] In his summary on the episcopacy Lightfoot claims that "under Cyprian the firm establishment of the bishopric took hold."[37] Yet in Cyprian's strong defense of the bishop, Lightfoot condemns him for the inception of the sacerdotal aspect of the episcopate.

The synod of Antioch intimated a regular custom of the people electing a bishop when it said, "If any bishop without a see shall throw himself upon a vacant church and seize its throne, without a full synod, he shall be cast out, even if all the people over whom he has usurped jurisdiction should choose him."[38] This shows that part of the appointment of the bishop was the election of the people. This was again clearly approved when it said, "If any bishop ordained to a parish shall not proceed to the parish to which he has been ordained, not through any fault of his own, but either because of the rejection of the people, or for any other reason not arising from himself, let him enjoy his rank and ministry."[39]

Being a strict student of the Scriptures, Jerome (380–420) discussed the relationship between the threefold office of the church in his time: "Lest any should in a spirit of contention argue that there must then have been more bishops than one in a single church, there is the following passage which clearly proves a bishop and a presbyter to be the same."[40] Jerome was a man of Scripture and thus sees that the later ecclesial establishment of the bishop was not in line with the Scripture, but nonetheless a tradition of the church that was kept to uproot heresies and maintain unity. In his commentary on Titus 1:5 he makes this clear: "With the ancients presbyters were the same as bishops;

36. Cyprian, *Epistles*, 370.
37. Lightfoot, "Christian Ministry," 258–59.
38. Percival, "Blessed and Holy Fathers," 116.
39. Percival, "Blessed and Holy Fathers," 117.
40. Jerome, *Letters*, 288.

but gradually all the responsibility was deferred to a single person, that the thickets of heresies might be rooted out. Therefore, as presbyters know that by the custom of the Church they are subject to him who shall have been set over them, so let bishops also be aware that they are superior to presbyters more owing to custom than to any actual ordinances of the Lord."[41]

In dialogue with Jerome, Augustine (354–430) also acknowledges that the distinction that was being drawn in their time between the elder and the overseer had come about, not because of apostolic teaching, but as the result of "the practice of the church."[42]

Implicitly validating the episcopacy, Pope Leo (400–461) left us with instruction on how the established office of bishop was to be appointed. He agreed with Cyprian that "no consideration permits men to be reckoned among bishops who have not been elected by the clergy, demanded by the laity, and consecrated by the bishops of the province with the assent of the metropolitan."[43] It is obvious that the normal practice of that time was that the bishop was to be a congregationally approved selection and not a behind-closed-doors selection by the elite. Leo showed that the bishop was to be well thought of within the congregation and known to have the prerequisites of ministry. Unfortunately this practice of congregationally approved and adequately qualified bishops was spurned by the later Catholic church during the medieval period.

Calvin summarized his views on the custom of the church by detaching the episcopacy from being understood as integral to the definition of a church. Instead he concluded that the true signs of the church were "wherever we see the Word of God purely preached and heard, and the sacraments administered according to Christ's institution."[44] In this he denies the claim by those of the Catholic or Anglo-Catholic persuasion who would deny the validity of the Presbyterian or Congregational church. In another place he condemns Rome's insistence on apostolic succession by

41. Jerome, *Commentaries*, 208.
42. Augustine, *Letters*, 361.
43. Leo, *Letters*, 110.
44. Calvin, *Institutes* (Battles), 1023.

condemning their pretense, revisionist history, and justification for their inexcusable doctrine, saying,

> They therefore revert to the point that they have the true church because from its beginning it has not been destitute of bishops, for one has followed another in unbroken succession. But what if I confront them with Greece? I therefore ask them once more why they say that the church perished among the Greeks, among whom the succession of bishops (in their opinion the sole custodian and preserver of the church) has never been interrupted. They make the Greeks schismatics; with what right? Because in withdrawing from the apostolic see, they lost their privilege. What? Would not they who fall away from Christ deserve to lose it much more? It therefore follows that this pretense of succession is vain unless their descendants conserve safe and uncorrupted the truth of Christ which they have received at their fathers' hands, and abide in it.[45]

Nonetheless, Calvin confirms the legitimacy of bishop as a distinct office. "There remain bishops and parish rectors. Would that they strove to preserve their office! For I willingly grant them that they have a godly and excellent office, if only they would fulfill it."[46] He ascribes the historical veracity of the episcopate for the sake of unity when he says, "All those to whom the office of teaching was enjoined they called presbyters. In each city these chose one of their number to whom they specially gave the title bishop in order that dissensions might not arise (as commonly happens) from equality of rank."[47] And again he shows the purpose of the bishop to fight discord: "A certain area was assigned to each city from which its presbyters were drawn, and it was thought of as belonging to the body of that church. Each college was under one bishop for the preservation of its organization and peace. While he surpassed the others in dignity, he was subject

45. Calvin, *Institutes* (Battles), 1043.
46. Calvin, *Institutes* (Battles), 1095.
47. Calvin, *Institutes* (Battles), 1069.

to the assembly of his brethren."[48] Thus he makes clear that the purpose of the bishop in the history of the church was to maintain unity, not to dominate. Calvin despised the episcopacy of his day and regarded it as nothing like the ancient custom, but rather filled with prelacy and sacerdotalism:

> Now all the people's right in electing a bishop has been taken away. Votes, assent, subscriptions, and all their like have vanished; the whole power has been transferred to the canons alone. They confer the episcopate on whom they please; they introduce him directly before the people, but to be adored, not to be examined. Yet Leo cries out that no reason allows this, and declares it a violent imposition. Cyprian, in testifying that only election by the people's consent flows from divine right, shows that the contrary custom conflicts with God's Word. Very many decrees of synods stringently forbid its being done otherwise, and, if it be done otherwise, declare it void. If these things are true, no canonical election remains today in the entire papacy either by divine or by ecclesiastical right.[49]

Calvin finally summarizes what he believes to be the most appropriate view of church governance that undergirded his entire presbyterian scheme:

> I mean that the Lord has in his sacred oracles faithfully embraced and clearly expressed both the whole sum of true righteousness, and all aspects of the worship of his majesty, and whatever was necessary to salvation; therefore, in these the Master alone is to be heard. But because he did not will in outward discipline and ceremonies to prescribe in detail what we ought to do (because he foresaw that this depended upon the state of the times, and he did not deem one form suitable for all ages), here we must take refuge in those general rules which he has given, that whatever the necessity of the church will require for order and decorum should be tested against

48. Calvin, *Institutes* (Battles), 1070.
49. Calvin, *Institutes* (Battles), 1085–86.

these. Lastly, because he has taught nothing specifically, and because these things are not necessary to salvation, and for the upbuilding of the church ought to be variously accommodated to the customs of each nation and age, it will be fitting (as the advantage of the church will require) to change and abrogate traditional practices and to establish new ones. Indeed, I admit that we ought not to charge into innovation rashly, suddenly, for insufficient cause. But love will best judge what may hurt or edify; and if we let love be our guide, all will be safe. Now it is the duty of Christian people to keep the ordinances that have been established according to this rule with a free conscience, indeed, without superstition, yet with a pious and ready inclination to obey; not to despise them, not to pass over them in careless negligence. So far ought we to be from openly violating them through pride and obstinacy! What sort of freedom of conscience could there be in such excessive attentiveness and caution? Indeed, it will be very clear when we consider that these are no fixed and permanent sanctions by which we are bound, but outward rudiments for human weakness. Although not all of us need them, we all use them, for we are mutually bound, one to another, to nourish mutual love. . . . Nevertheless, the established custom of the region, or humanity itself and the rule of modesty, dictate what is to be done or avoided in these matters. In them a man commits no crime if out of imprudence or forgetfulness he departs from them; but if out of contempt, this willfulness is to be disapproved. Similarly, the days themselves, the hours, the structure of the places of worship, what psalms are to be sung on what day, are matters of no importance. But it is convenient to have definite days and stated hours, and a place suitable to receive all, if there is any concern for the preservation of peace. For confusion in such details would become the seed of great contentions if every man were allowed, as he pleased, to change matters affecting public order! For it will never happen that the same thing will please all if matters are regarded as indifferent and left to individual choice. But if anyone loudly complains and wishes here to be wiser than he ought, let him see with what reason he can defend his overscrupulousness before the Lord.[50]

The Anglican archbishop James Ussher advocated for a mixture of presbyterian and episcopal governance during the seventeenth century when tensions were high between both forms of government. "[Ussher's proposal] could have been interpreted even by radical puritans in early 1641 as a satisfactory decentralization of episcopal power. During the 1650s, indeed, Baxter and other presbyterians could see in it a government in which the bishop was essentially a moderator among equals."[51] In this proposal Ussher advocated for weekly meetings of local congregation elders, annual meetings of elders from various congregations, along with an annual national assembly. By doing this he defended the historic practice of presbyterian governance while at the same time he advocated for a moderate form of episcopacy. However, his proposal failed because of the dissent of the extremists on both sides of the issue. It is interesting to note that Ussher was appointed to participate in the Westminster Assembly in 1647, thus showing his involvement with the standards supporting the Presbyterian churches today.

More recent studies on the structure of church governance show the spectrum of reasonable assertions for an episcopal form of governance. Toon speaks about the development of the episcopacy: "We have to accept that our knowledge of the church and how it was actually organized locally is minimal from the apostolic age until the end of the second century. . . . Apparently, however, by circa AD 200 such hierarchy was in place virtually everywhere. . . . Elected by the church membership, the bishop was usually ordained/consecrated by existing bishops."[52] The *bene esse* of the episcopal form of governance is given by Zahl when he says, "The threefold order of ministry that culminates in the order of bishops is intended to sustain and safeguard the church's catholicity. The

---

50. Calvin, *Institutes*, 1208–10.

51. Abbott, "James Ussher," 244.

52. Cowan, *4 Views*, 26.

church's catholicity consists in its preaching of the pure Word of God and its faithful administration of the two Bible or 'gospel' sacraments: Baptism and Holy Communion."[53]

Taking all of these historical precedents into account, unity seems to have been at the forefront in the innovation of the ecclesial office of bishop. It seems to have worked well for much of church history, but was slowly abused until it ultimately devolved into prelacy and sacerdotalism. However, since it would be improper to "throw the baby out with the bath water," there remains an opportunity to utilize a moderated episcopacy as a means for a unifying regional approach to governance. Again the drive for an episcopal form of governance over evangelical churches is less about the *esse* and more about the *bene esse* of our particular context within the church. It need not be the abused version that caused undue subjugation of laity in the past. A moderated form of episcopalianism does not need to move into Erastianism and can also offset the bad influence of extreme congregationalism.

In the end, Allison gives credence to this creativity and flexibility saying, "Churches in the third millennium have been challenged to consider seriously how they should be governed. While several diverse polities have characterized church history, new issues are giving rise to a growing number of new models of government in the contemporary scene. Relying on Scripture and tradition, together with cultural developments from both religious and secular sources, churches are changing how they are governed in unprecedented ways."[54]

Theological Precedents

Before proceeding to practicals, we must first analyze one of the root issues regarding church polity—namely, the distinction between the regulative and normative principle of worship. The regulative principle of worship is the perspective that Christians ought to limit

---

53. Brand and Stanton, *Perspectives*, 239.
54. Allison, *Historical Theology*, 610.

themselves to what is expressly subscribed in the Scriptures, while the normative principle of worship is the perspective that Christians are free to worship in any way that is not expressly forbidden by the Scripture. As we have seen previously, an episcopal form of governance finds itself well within the bounds of such a conversation. While it is not commanded in Scripture, it is also not expressly forbidden. It will be my goal to show why a normative principle of worship is necessary for a moderated episcopacy.

Frame winsomely advocates for a regulative principle in a way that aligns with the traditional understanding of the normative principle: "Actions that are neither forbidden nor commanded are permitted (1 Cor. 7:6). What God permits us to do is good. So actions in this category are good, not bad or indifferent."[55] Thus Frame stands solidly within the normative camp while stealing the term "regulative" from its traditional understanding. He even extends the regulative principle beyond worship to all ethical decisions. Whereas some have placed certain doctrines under the umbrella of adiaphora (i.e., things indifferent), Frame says this is impossible. He concludes that there are a number of valid reasons that adiaphora became so popular and summarizes these valid points without labeling them "indifferent." He agrees that when making a choice between two or more good things "our choice is good, not indifferent."[56] Concerning those things about which Scripture does not speak specifically, he regards that the Scripture speaks generally and implicitly about all things, and thus any action "is either ethically good or ethically bad, for it is either to God's glory or not."[57] Having placed all of life under the regulative principle of worship, Frame discusses how one is to take general principles from the Scripture and make decisions through their God-given reason. "God gives general principles, and we seek to apply these principles."[58] He adds, "When God reveals his will at a general level, we should try to implement

55. Frame, *Doctrine of the Christian Life*, 169.
56. Frame, *Doctrine of the Christian Life*, 169.
57. Frame, *Doctrine of the Christian Life*, 169.
58. Frame, *Doctrine of the Christian Life*, 475.

the specifics by our sanctified human wisdom."[59] And again, "His commands cover everything we do . . . the proper applications of these commands, however, require human thought, consideration of the broader principles of Scripture, and the work of the Holy Spirit in our hearts."[60]

To help with his argument he discusses the classic Reformed distinction between *elements* and *circumstances*. "Elements are those aspects of worship that Scripture commands. Circumstances are those things we must do in order to perform the elements."[61] Using Frame's ethical framework, church polity can also be included in this conversation.[62] Since episcopal government is not prohibited, then it is to be commended. But we must use our wisdom to decide whether this structure is the most helpful, or most in line with the *bene esse* of the church.

Turretin concludes, "Although we believe that the presbyterian order and parity or equality of pastors received among us approaches nearer to the institution of Christ and the apostles and the practice of the apostolic church, still we are unwilling to disturb anyone on this subject or to condemn the usage of the evangelical and Reformed churches, who retain the episcopal government so far, as more suitable to the genius and morals and political form of government of their people and more useful for good order and the exercise of discipline . . . and this order be acknowledged as of ecclesiastical, not of divine right."[63]

The Westminster standard leaves wiggle room concerning the government of the church when it says within the first chapter, "There are some circumstances concerning the worship of God, and government of the Church, common to human actions and societies, which are to be ordered by the light of nature and Christian prudence."[64]

59. Frame, *Doctrine of the Christian Life*, 480.
60. Frame, *Doctrine of the Christian Life*, 481.
61. Frame, *Doctrine of the Christian Life*, 464.
62. Frame, *Doctrine of the Christian Life*, 474.
63. Turretin, *Institutes*, 3:209.
64. Westminster Assembly, *Westminster Confession*, 18–19.

To his presbyterian brothers who claim the episcopacy is not warranted because of insufficient grounds in the Scripture, Murray retorts,

> It should be recognized that there is much in the form of organization and procedure adopted in presbyterian churches that cannot plead the authority of the New Testament. And the reason why certain forms of organization and procedure have been adopted and practiced, which cannot plead the prescription or warrant of Scripture itself, is simply the recognition that there are some circumstances concerning the worship of God and government of the church which are to be ordered by the light of nature and Christian prudence, in accord with the general principles of the Word of God. Much in the actual polity of the church falls into this category and we must guard against the notion that differences in the form of organization, and particularly in mode of procedure, necessarily violate the biblical principle of presbyterian government. There is much room for variety, and the church of Christ is always under the necessity of devising and adopting better forms or procedure and organization than those which tradition may have established.[65]

And he also challenges the congregational view when he questions, "Are we to suppose that in the government of the church now and ever since the death of the apostles, corporate government no longer exists? Are we to suppose that every unit of the church of Christ exists governmentally in complete independence of all other units, and directs its affairs under the supervision of no other hierarchy than the supreme headship of Christ and the delegated canonicity of the apostles? If the answer is in the affirmative, we must recognize the complete change that took place with the death of the apostles."[66] By making these claims Murray advocates for a presbyterian government at the very least, but does not close the door on episcopal government.

---

65. Murray, *Select Lectures*, 349.
66. Murray, *Select Lectures*, 343.

As previously mentioned, the stance of this book is not that an episcopal form of governance is of the essence of the church, but rather is for the well being of the church. The unity and order of the apostolic church under the rule of local elders is of first importance. However, the government that accomplishes this can be found in the episcopal, presbyterian, and congregational forms. But which is more in line with the *bene esse* of the church? It is my position that a moderated episcopal approach to governance promises to be the most unifying form of government for conservative evangelicals in our twenty-first-century, highly individualized, fragmented, and polarized America.

First Steps

So how can such a process start? As the analogy goes, "You can't steer a parked car." There are many opportunities that can only be discovered through action. After first referencing previous attempts in this endeavour, I would like to suggest some small steps to take toward this evangelical ecumenical ecclesiology.

In his attempt for evangelical ecumenism as a minister within the Reformed Episcopal tradition, Shields asked, "Why not build up a general confederation in some grand national council of denominations, a sort of Congress of the United Churches of the United States, having its senate of bishops as the conservative element, and its house of presbyters as the progressive element, with its ratio of Congregational representation and its legislation restricted to domestic charities and foreign missions?"[67] This is an audacious goal, and is not the most appropriate "first step." Nonetheless his ecumenical spirit makes such a dream possible. To quell any fear that the presbyterian or congregationalist would have, he adds, "Historic episcopacy has ever included congregational and presbyterian spheres of the church organism, and as locally adapted to the civil and religious institutions of this

---

67. Shields, *Historic Episcopate*, 6.

country, will neither sacrifice the liberties of the congregation, nor the right of the presbytery."[68]

Aligned with Shields's perspective, the inception of the Reformed Episcopal Churches in the United States was devoted to the union of all evangelicalism. In his survey, Platt includes the perspective of Rev. William Freemantle as a particularly noteworthy representative of this movement:

> This Church is comprehensive. This appears in the union of Episcopal oversight with parochial self-government; in the provision for baptism by sprinkling, pouring or immersion; in the recognition in both theory and practice of the absolute validity of all properly constituted ministries and in the consequent recognition of the regularity of the membership of all Christian Churches. Such members are invariably invited to the Lord's Table, and in uniting with this Church, need not be confirmed except at their own request.[69]

Unfortunately, due to the rising influence of theological liberalism in the early twentieth century, this movement pulled back in fear of liberal intrusion:

> By withdrawing from these ecumenical contacts the church reinforced its strict attitudes on the need and function of conservative theology and expanded the significance of those doctrinal elements—inerrancy of Scripture, vicarious atonement, the divinity of Christ and the reality of his resurrection, and the truth of the creeds—which informed its existence and defined its purpose. Purged of extraneous associations, the church resolved to pursue a witness to what it understood as the divine will for it. The ecumenical aspirations present in its founding and palpably evident in the church's activity from 1908 through the early 1930s were discarded when they failed to reflect and buttress the church's own doctrinal stance. The sympathies with ecumenism and interchurch fellowship waned in the face of theological

68. Shields, *Historic Episcopate*, 37.
69. Platt, "Ecumenism," 324.

relativism and doctrinal liberalism which were increasingly perceived as compromising the church's own integrity and probity.[70]

Why did they not attempt to expand the significance of conservative theology within a continuing initiative of conservative evangelical ecumenism? One of Satan's best tools is to divide, and it seems they gave into his ploys as a result of fear or apathy. The narrow road to glory is narrow because it is filled with difficulty. Wide and easy is the road that leads to division and destruction. The road of ecumenism is narrow and difficult indeed, but it is a road that ends in glory.

One small step to take in order to begin this moderated form of episcopal governance among evangelical churches is to host a monthly meeting with various pastors in a particular area in order to:

1. Share evidence of God's grace within their own ministry.

2. Discuss barriers to ministry within the community.

3. Share ideas for evangelism and prepare evangelistic events together.

4. Discuss ways to promote the Christian causes in their local government.

5. Coordinate fundraisers for Christian organizations.

6. Pray with one another.

Perhaps these would be small steps that could organically evolve into formal confederations. These are just a few ideas; what is important is that church leaders provide the environment needed to grow the idea that conservative evangelical churches ought to practice a moderated episcopal approach to governance.

70. Platt, "Ecumenism," 343.

Conclusion

I HOPE THAT THIS book has given a reasonable view as to why and how credobaptist and credocommunion churches ought to sanction *the theological concept* of presumed regeneration and *the theological practices* of paedobaptism and paedocommunion. This does not mean that members of each church *must* adhere to the concept of presumed regeneration or practice paedobaptism and paedocommunion, but rather that it ought be sanctioned as an orthodox interpretation of the Scriptures without incurring denigration or formal discipline from the credo faction. This seems to be at least one of the primary causes of division in conservative evangelical churches and it shows much promise if enacted. Rather than Baptist churches that withhold membership or eldership from those of the paedobaptist persuasion, or Presbyterian churches that withhold eldership from those of the paedocommunion persuasion, there remains an opportunity to unify on the fundamentals of the faith while allowing freedom of conscience as it pertains to non-fundamental issues. There is a way forward in which Christians can link arms in order to protect themselves from enemy forces. The acceptance of these theological premises would provide the motivation and humility needed to address the tricky issue of church governance. While the polity presented above is what I deem to be the most ideal, I recognize that there are better minds than myself who may be able to create another type of governing structure that accomplishes the same goal of conservative evangelical unity, and to that I give a hearty "Praise

God!" If this book can be used to generate conservative evangelical ecumenism in local pockets around this country then I would be satisfied. My fundamental goal in writing this book is that the conversation would move forward and be deemed a worthy one in which to participate.

Keep the Main Things the Main Thing

Understandably, much of what was discussed in this book may seem novel to many readers and initially feel inappropriate. I felt the same way when I heard some of these perspectives. I was concerned that if I affirmed any sort of ecumenical approach to theology that I would begin a slippery slope into subjectivism and "evan-jellyfish" theology. What's next—the Sparkle Creed?! Ecumenism was just a code word for "no backbone" or "wokeism." But the more that I opened my ear to others on less important doctrinal issues, the more I became convinced on the fundamentals of the faith. My Trinitarianism and Christology are more precious to me now then they ever have been. These fundamentals of the faith that once seemed so basic for any believer have become increasingly awe-inspiring and captivating. And this was only made possible by listening to the different perspectives of those other members of the body of Christ. Those of other theological persuasions within the same household of God are not my enemies but rather are part of the beautiful tapestry that God is weaving together that he calls his church. And though we should not limit ourselves to only the fundamentals of the faith, these fundamentals form the foundation for fruitful conversation on every other doctrine contained within the Scriptures. It is not an exaggeration to say that the strength of one's Trinitarianism and Christology corresponds directly with one's maturity and faithful exegesis of the Scriptures.

In this polarized world that highlights differences and minimizes agreement, the church needs to be the city on the hill that highlights agreements and works through its differences like a healthy family. In consideration of the millions of saints who make up the church of Christ through the ages, it takes only a small amount of humility to recognize that one's interpretation of the Scripture might not be perfect. And once this admission is made it is only a small step toward ecumenism. The word *ecumenism* finds its etymological roots in the Greek word οἰκουμένη meaning "the whole inhabited world." Its basic root meaning conveys a meaning of "household" (οἶκος).[1] And since the church is the household of God (Eph 2:19; 1 Tim 3:15; 1 Pet 4:17) and ought not be divided because a house divided against itself cannot stand (Luke 11:17), then it should not be difficult for each Christian to desire ecumenism. The church should not settle for amicable divorces but should show sibling love and outdo one another in showing honor (Rom 12:10). The only way forward is to keep the main things the main thing. Focus on those doctrines that have united the church through the ages and that were formulated in those ancient creeds (Apostles', Nicene, and Athanasian).

Destruction of Denominations

I started this book with my own painful experience of denominationalism. For seven and a half years I was denied membership to a Bible-believing evangelically conservative church because of my view on baptism. I am happy to say that this stalemate has ended and this church has gladly welcomed me as a voting member in their church family! This decision did not come without pain though. There were some families of the church who resigned their membership due to the decision, but the vast majority of the church was happy to band together in the name of Christ for the sake of his kingdom. This shows that there will be trials and pain for those who desire this conservative evangelical ecumenism. But the Lord told us that trials would attend the lives of his faithful who seek to live on mission according to his word in a spirit of love. My church has endured the pain of the breakup largely due to its focus on mission and ministry rather than secondary doctrinal squabbles.

1. Brannan, *Lexham Analytical Lexicon.*

It is lamentable that the church is divided. "Somewhere in each of our hearts ought to be the conviction that denominations should work, not to their own glorification, but to their own extinction."[2] Perhaps the source of this denominationalism is pride. Perhaps the division has simply grown far enough apart that a sense of comfort in division is at play. Or perhaps we have forgotten the simple command that our Lord gave us in 1 John 4:21: "Whoever loves God must also love his brother." How can we claim to love our brother while separating our fellowship from him? I never want to experience a life within the church apart from my Baptist brethren. Especially considering that my future in heaven is one in which we will praise Jesus Christ as Lord with one voice in close proximity. I am aware that there are flaws in my analysis that will need to be ironed out, but you cannot steer a parked car. I hope that this book will have inspired a conviction in the reader to attempt a movement in their own little circle toward a conservative evangelical ecumenism. Though the road is sure to be long and rocky at times, the view at the top of the mountain is just as our Lord promised. And it is the sure path to characterizing the "city on the hill" that proclaims our Trinitarian God to a lost and dying world. I finish the book with an exhortation from a beloved role model of mine, Baptist pastor John Bunyan: "May the time soon arrive when water shall not quench love, but when all the churches militant shall form one army, with one object,—that of extending the Redeemer's kingdom."[3]

2. Frame, *Evangelical Reunion*, 28.

3. Bunyan, *Differences in Judgment*, 32.

Bibliography

Abbott, William M. "James Ussher and 'Ussherian' Episcopacy, 1640–1656: The Primate and His Reduction Manuscript." *Albion* 22:2 (1990) 237–59.

Allison, Gregg R. *Historical Theology: An Introduction to Christian Doctrine.* Grand Rapids: Zondervan Academic, 2011.

Atwater, Lyman Hotchkiss. *The Children of the Church and Sealing Ordinances.* Philadelphia: Presbyterian Board of Publication, 1858.

Augustine. *The Enchiridion.* Translated by J. F. Shaw. In vol. 3 of *The Nicene and Post-Nicene Fathers,* series 1, edited by Philip Schaff, 229–76. Buffalo: Christian Literature, 1887.

———. "Letter 138 (A.D. 412)." Translated by J. G. Cunningham. From vol. 1 of *The Nicene and Post-Nicene Fathers,* series 1, edited by Philip Schaff. Buffalo: Christian Literature, 1887. Revised and edited for New Advent by Kevin Knight. https://www.newadvent.org/fathers/1102138.htm.

———. *Letters of St. Augustine.* Translated by J. G. Cunningham. In vol. 1 of *The Nicene and Post-Nicene Fathers,* series 1, edited by Philip Schaff, 209–593. Buffalo: Christian Literature, 1887.

———. *Sermons 148–183.* Edited by John E. Rotelle, translated by Edmund Hill. Pt. 3, vol. 5 of *The Works of Saint Augustine: A Translation for the 21st Century.* New Rochelle, NY: New City, 1992.

Bradshaw, Paul F., et al., trans. and eds. *The Apostolic Tradition: A Commentary.* Minneapolis: Fortress, 2002.

Brand, Chad, and Norman R. Stanton. *Perspectives on Church Government: Five Views of Church Polity.* Nashville: Baker Academic, 2004.

Brannan, Rick. *The Lexham Analytical Lexicon to the Greek New Testament.* Rev. ed. Logos Research Systems, 2008–2013. Logos digital.

Bruce, F. F. *Commentary on the Book of the Acts: The English Text with Introduction, Exposition and Notes.* Grand Rapids: Eerdmans, 1954.

Bunyan, John. *Differences in Judgment About Water-Baptism, No Bar to Communion* [. . .]. London: John Wilkins, 1673.

Calvin, John. *1554–1558*. Edited by Jules Bonnet, translated by Marcus Robert Gilchrist. Vol. 6, pt. 3 of *Selected Works of John Calvin: Tracts and Letters*, edited by Henry Beveridge and Jules Bonnet. Albany, OR: Books for the Ages, 1998. https://media.sabda.org/alkitab-7/LIBRARY/CALVIN/CAL_SLW6.PDF.

———. *Acts of the Council of Trent with the Antidote*. 1547. https://www.monergism.com/thethreshold/sdg/calvin_trentantidote.html.

———. *Commentary on the Epistle of Paul to the Philippians*. Edited by David W. Torrance and Thomas F. Torrance, translated by John W. Fraser. Grand Rapids: Baker, 2003.

———. *Institutes of the Christian Religion*. Edited by John T. McNeill, translated by Ford Lewis Battles. Vol. 1. Library of Christian Classics. Louisville: Westminster John Knox, 2011.

———. *Institutes of the Christian Religion*. Translated by Henry Beveridge. Peabody, MA: Hendrickson, 2008.

———. *Sermons on Genesis: Chapters 1–11*. Translated by Rob Roy McGregor. Edinburgh: Banner of Truth Trust, 2009.

Chapell, Bryan. "A Pastoral Overview of Infant Baptism." In *The Case for Covenantal Infant Baptism*, edited by Gregg Strawbridge, 9–29. Phillipsburg, NJ: P&R, 2003.

Clement of Rome. *The First Epistle of Clement to the Corinthians*. Translated by John Keith. In vol. 9 of *The Ante-Nicene Fathers*, edited by Allan Menzies, 229–48. Buffalo: Christian Literature, 1896.

Communion of Reformed Evangelical Churches. *Governing Documents*. Last revised April 6, 2022. https://crechurches.org/wp-content/uploads/2024/04/CREC_Governing_Docs_2022.pdf.

Cowan, Steven. *Who Runs the Church? 4 Views on Church Government*. Grand Rapids: Zondervan, 2004.

Cyprian of Carthage. *The Epistles of Cyprian*. Translated by Robert Ernest Wallis. In vol. 5 of *The Ante-Nicene Fathers*, edited by Alexander Roberts et al., 275–409. Buffalo: Christian Literature, 1886.

Dewey, Orville. *Letters of an English Traveller to His Friend in England, on the "Revivals of Religion" in America*. London: G&J Robinson, 1828.

Ferguson, Everett. *Baptism in the Early Church: History, Theology, and Liturgy in the First Five Centuries*. Grand Rapids: Eerdmans, 2009.

———. "Sacraments in the Pre-Nicene Period." In *The Oxford Handbook of Sacramental Theology*, edited by Hans Boersma and Matthew Levering, 158–78. Oxford: Oxford University Press, 2015.

Fitzgerald, Allan D., ed. *Augustine Through the Ages: An Encyclopedia*. Grand Rapids: Eerdmans, 1999.

Forbes, Greg W. *1 Peter*. Exegetical Guide to the Greek New Testament. Nashville: B&H, 2014.

Frame, John. *The Doctrine of the Christian Life*. Phillipsburg, NJ: P&R, 2008.

———. *Evangelical Reunion*. Grand Rapids: Baker, 1991.

————. "Some Questions About the Regulative Principle." *Westminster Theological Journal* 54:2 (1992) 357–66.

Gibson, David. "'Fathers of Faith, My Fathers Now!': On Abraham, Covenant, and the Theology of Paedobaptism." *Themelios* 40:1 (2015) 14–34.

Grassmick, John D., et al., eds. NET Bible. Full notes ed. Nashville: Thomas Nelson, 2019.

Hatch, Nathan. *The Democratization of American Christianity.* New Haven: Yale University Press, 1989.

Hodge, Charles. "The Church Membership of Infants." *Biblical Repertory and Princeton Review* 30 (1858) 347–89.

————. "Review of Discourses on Christian Nurture by Horace Bushnell." *Biblical Repertory and Princeton Review* 19 (1847) 520–21.

————. *Soteriology.* Vol. 3 of *Systematic Theology.* Peabody: Hendrickson, 2020.

Holmes, Michael W., ed. and trans. *The Apostolic Fathers in English.* Grand Rapids: Baker Academic, 2006.

Horton, Michael. *Pilgrim Theology: Core Doctrines for Christian Disciples.* Grand Rapids: Zondervan Academic, 2012.

Ignatius of Antioch. *The Epistle of Ignatius to the Philadelphians.* In vol. 1 of *Ante-Nicene Fathers,* edited and translated by Alexander Roberts and James Donaldson, 79–85. Buffalo: Christian Literature, 1885.

————. *The Epistle of Ignatius to the Smyrnaeans.* In vol. 1 of *Ante-Nicene Fathers,* edited and translated by Alexander Roberts and James Donaldson, 86–92. Buffalo: Christian Literature, 1885.

Irenaeus. *Against Heresies.* In vol. 1 of *Ante-Nicene Fathers,* edited and translated by Alexander Roberts and James Donaldson, 309–567. Buffalo: Christian Literature, 1885.

Jeremias, Joachim. *Infant Baptism in the First Four Centuries.* Translated by David Cairns. London: SCM, 1960. Repr., Eugene, OR: Wipf & Stock, 2004.

Jerome. *The Letters of St. Jerome.* Translated by W. H. Fremantle et al. In vol. 6 of *The Nicene and Post-Nicene Fathers,* series 2, edited by Philip Schaff and Henry Wace, 1–295. New York: Christian Literature, 1893.

————. *St. Jerome's Commentaries on Galatians, Titus, and Philemon.* Translated by Thomas P. Scheck. Notre Dame: University of Notre Dame Press, 2010.

Keidel, Christian. "Is the Lord's Supper for Children?" *Westminster Theological Journal* 37:3 (1975) 301–41.

Kelly, J. N. D. *Early Christian Doctrines.* 4th ed. Edinburgh: R&R Clark, 1968.

Kuyper, Abraham. "Calvinism and Confessional Revision." In vol. 3 of *The Presbyterian and Reformed Review,* edited by Benjamin B. Warfield et al., 369–99. New York: Randolph, 1891.

Ladd, George Eldon. *A Theology of the New Testament.* Grand Rapids: Eerdmans, 1974.

Leithart, Peter J. "Infant Baptism in History: An Unfinished Tragicomedy." In *The Case for Covenantal Infant Baptism*, edited by Gregg Strawbridge, 246–62. Phillipsburg, NJ: P&R, 2003.

Leo the Great. *Letters*. Translated by Charles Lett Feltoe. In vol. 12 of *The Nicene and Post-Nicene Fathers*, series 2, edited by Philip Schaff and Henry Wace, 1–114. New York: Christian Literature, 1895.

Lightfoot, J. B. "The Christian Ministry." In *Saint Paul's Epistle to the Philippians*, 181–269. 4th ed. London: Macmillan, 1878.

Lusk, Richard. "Covenant and Election FAQs." Theologia, 2002. http://hornes. org/theologia/rich-lusk/covenant-election-faqs.

———. *Paedofaith: A Primer on the Mystery of Infant Salvation and a Handbook for Covenant Parents*. Monroe, LA: Athanasius, 2005.

Luther, Martin. *Word and Sacrament II*. Edited by Abdel Ross Wentz, translated by Frederick C. Ahrens. Vol. 36 of *Luther's Works*. Philadelphia: Fortress, 1959.

Mather, Cotton. *A Family Well-Ordered*. Morgan, PA: Soli Deo Gloria, 2001.

Meyers, Jeffrey J. "Presbyterian, Examine Thyself: Restoring Children to the Table." In *The Case for Covenant Communion*, edited by Gregg Strawbridge, 19–34. Monroe, LA: Athanasius, 2006.

Murray, John. *Select Lectures in Systematic Theology*. Vol. 2 of *The Collected Writings of John Murray*. East Peoria, IL: Versa, 2017.

Nicoletti, Stephen. "The History of Credocommunion: From the Early Church Until 1500." *Bantam Review* 1 (2012) 19–38.

Percival, Henry, ed. "The Canons of the 318 Holy Fathers Assembled in the City of Nice, in Bithynia." In vol. 14 of *The Nicene and Post-Nicene Fathers*, series 2, edited by Philip Schaff and Henry Wace, 8–45. New York: Scribner's Sons, 1900.

———, ed. "The Canons of the Blessed and Holy Fathers Assembled at Antioch in Syria," In vol. 14 of *The Nicene and Post-Nicene Fathers*, series 2, edited by Philip Schaff and Henry Wace, 108–21. New York: Scribner's Sons, 1900.

———, ed. "The Canons of the One Hundred and Fifty Fathers Who Assembled at Constantinople," In vol. 14 of *The Nicene and Post-Nicene Fathers*, series 2, edited by Philip Schaff and Henry Wace, 172–86. New York: Scribner's Sons, 1900.

Platt, Warren C. "Ecumenism and the Reformed Episcopal Church: An Analysis of Its Development from the Late Nineteenth Century Until 1945." *Anglican and Episcopal History* 57:3 (1988) 320–44.

Rayburn, Robert S. "A Presbyterian Defense of Paedocommunion." In *The Case for Covenant Communion*, edited by Gregg Strawbridge, 3–18. Monroe, LA: Athanasius, 2006.

Robertson, O. Palmer. *The Christ of the Covenants*. Phillipsburg, NJ: P&R, 1980.

Schenck, Lewis. *The Presbyterian Doctrine of Children in the Covenant*. Phillipsburg, NJ: P&R, 1940.

Shields, Charles Woodruff. *Historic Episcopate: An Essay on the Four Articles of Church Unity Proposed by the American House of Bishops and the Lambeth Conference.* New York: Scribner's Sons, 1894.

Stander, H. F., and J. P. Louw. *Baptism in the Early Church.* Leeds: Reformation Today Trust, 2004.

Strawbridge, Gregg, ed. *The Case for Covenant Communion.* Monroe, LA: Athanasius, 2006.

———, ed. *The Case for Covenantal Infant Baptism.* Phillipsburg, NJ: P&R, 2003.

Trouwborst, Thomas. "From Covenant to Chaos: The Reformers and Their Heirs on Covenant Succession." In *To You and Your Children: Examining the Biblical Doctrine of Covenant Succession*, edited by Benjamin K. Wikner, 59–105. Moscow, ID: Canon, 2005.

Turretin, Francis. *Institutes of Elenctic Theology.* Edited by James T. Dennison Jr. and translated by George Musgrave Geiger. 3 vols. Phillipsburg, NJ: P&R, 1997.

Tertullian. *A Treatise on the Soul (De Anima).* Translated by Peter Holmes. In vol. 3 of *The Ante-Nicene Fathers*, edited by Alexander Roberts et al., 181–235. Buffalo: Christian Literature, 1885.

Ursinus, Zacharias. *The Commentary of Dr. Zacharias Ursinus on the Heidelberg Catechism.* Translated by G. W. Williard. Columbus: Scott & Bascom, 1852.

Vincent, Marvin R. *Word Studies in the New Testament.* 4 vols. Grand Rapids: Eerdmans, 1946.

Warfield, Benjamin B. "The Polemics of Infant Baptism." In *Studies in Theology*, 477–505. Carlisle, PA: Banner of Truth, 1988.

Warner, Anna Bartlett. "Jesus Loves Me, This I Know." Hymnary, 1859. https://hymnary.org/text/jesus_loves_me_this_i_know_for_the_bible.

Westminster Assembly. *The Westminster Confession of Faith.* Edinburgh ed. Philadelphia: Young, 1851.

Witsius, Hermann. "On the Efficacy and Utility of Baptism in the Case of Elect Infants Whose Parents Are Under the Covenant." Translated by William Marshall, edited by J. Mark Beach. *Mid-America Journal of Theology* 17 (2006) 121–90.

www.ingramcontent.com/pod-product-compliance
Lightning Source LLC
Chambersburg PA
CBHW052153090426
42741CB00010B/2254